Thinking About Quality

• • • • •

Thinking About Quality

Progress, Wisdom,
and the Deming Philosophy

* * * * * * * * *
* * * * * * * * * *
* * * * * * * * *

Lloyd Dobyns and Clare Crawford-Mason

* * * * *

TIMES BOOKS

RANDOM HOUSE

There are numerous community quality groups, Deming study groups and teachers and consultants who served as facilitators at Deming seminars. There are also books and videotapes about the Deming method. For information call (301) 588-4095.

Copyright © 1994 by Lloyd Dobyns and
Clare Crawford Mason
All rights reserved under International and Pan-American Copyright Conventions.
Published in the United States by Times Books, a division of Random House, Inc., New York, and simultaneously in Canada by Random House of Canada Limited, Toronto.

Library of Congress Cataloging-in-Publication Data

Dobyns, Lloyd.
Thinking about quality : progress, wisdom, and the Deming philosophy / Lloyd Dobyns & Clare Crawford-Mason.
p.   cm.
Includes bibliographical references.
ISBN 8129-2133-X
1. Quality control.   2. Total quality management.
3. Industrial management.   I. Crawford-Mason, Clare.
II. Title.
TS156.D615   1994
658.5'62—dc20   93-32402

Book design by Rebecca Aidlin

Manufactured in the United States of America
9   7   6   8

* * * * *

In Appreciation of W. Edwards Deming

(October 14, 1900—December 20, 1993)

W. Edwards Deming was a revolutionary living in revolutionary times. During his life, the world changed completely, but that still was not enough change for him. He wanted us to change not only what we do, but how we think and live as well.

Nearly everything that we accept as an ordinary convenience of the twentieth century—electricity, television, vacuum cleaner, automobile, airplane—did not exist when W. Edwards Deming was born in the closing days of the nineteenth century. Most modern consumer products were all invented during his lifetime, and some of them are better made and more valuable now because of him. He did not invent or discover quality, but he did recognize how it could be achieved and then developed a management system to produce quality at a reasonable cost. More than that, adopting his system is making us change what we believe as we go into the twenty-first century.

Deming was born October 14, 1900, the same year the Paris Metro opened and ground was broken for the New York subway system, the first Zeppelin trial flights were held, and two birds—the passenger pigeon and the Caracara hawk—became extinct. Perhaps two thousand foreigners died in the Boxer Rebellion in China in 1900, but about six thousand Texans died in a hurricane at Galveston that September, still the worst natural disaster in American history. Hawaii became a territory that year, and the nation went on the gold standard; that is, you could redeem paper dollars for gold.

Deming was one of the forty well-known people we can identify who were born that year. Three survive— Walter Lantz, the cartoonist who created Woody Woodpecker, Lawrence Spivak, the co-founder and long-time moderator of "Meet the Press," and the Queen Mother. The other thirty-seven born in 1900, when life expectancy for the American male was forty-seven years, have died. Deming is the most recent. The writer Thomas Wolfe died in 1938, sixteen days short of his thirty-eighth brithday. By contrast, the Romanian-born film director Jean Negulesco was ninety-three when he died in July. He's rather interesting, since he directed both *Johnny Belinda*, a sensitive and successful film, and *The Rains of Ranchipur*, which ranks as one of the worst films Hollywood ever made. You have to wonder how one man could do that.

Representative Claude Pepper (D.-Fla.) was eighty-seven when he died in Washington, D.C., where he was recognized as *the* champion of the elderly in Congress.

Others from that year (and the year each died) included Mabel Mercer (1984) and Helen Morgan ('41), singers who set standards only a few have matched. Heinrich Himmler ('45) and the Ayatollah Khomeini ('89) set their own standards as well, but of a different kind. Helen Hayes ('93) and Spencer Tracy ('67) were not only famous actors, they were among the finest as well. Depending on your own interests (and your age, we suppose), you may or may not remember Polly Adler ('62), Louis Armstrong ('71), Taylor Caldwell ('85), Aaron Copland ('90), Erich Fromm ('80), Margaret Mitchell ('49), Lord Louis Mountbatten ('76), Louise Nevelson ('88), Ernie Pyle ('45), Hyman Rickover ('86), and Adlai Stevenson ('65). Good as all those people are and were at what they did, not one has matched the contribution to the world that Deming has made. True, Khomeini was a revolutionary, but Deming was a *world* revolutionary.

The irony is that Deming was the only one not found in standard lists of well-known people. Until he was seventy-nine, he was known in academic circles, but unknown to the general American public. He has sixteen honorary doctorate degrees, but only one—from his alma mater, the University of Wyoming—was presented before 1981. After that, the honorary degree storm broke—almost one a year (none in '84, '90, and '92), two in '83 and '93, *four* in '91. Yale gave him a Doctor of Laws degree that year, and Harvard followed in 1993, the same year that university made chef Julia Child a Doctor of Humane Letters. Two more colleges had announced before his death that they would give Deming honorary doctorates in the spring of '94.

The turning point between academic obscurity and public fame was Tuesday, June 24, 1980. At 9:30 EDT that night, NBC News aired a 90-minute television documentary *If Japan Can . . . Why Can't We?* It explored comparative productivity and tried to explain why Japan was beginning to do better economically than was the United States, and one of the people featured was W. Edwards Deming, who had taught his quality system to the Japanese. Starting the next day, his phone rang constantly. Television, which he didn't watch, made Deming famous.

We both worked on that program, and the questions we asked Deming in several interviews forced him to think about what he had done and was doing. To make us understand, he had to explain his system simply and directly.

Until he died, we continued to ask him questions in interviews and over monthly Saturday night dinners of lobster and corn on the cob, his favorite meal. At one of those dinners in Washington in the mid-1980's, pressed to say what made the difference in Japan, a question he had always avoided, Deming drew himself to his full seated height, slapped his hand on the table, and said firmly and finally, "One lone man with profound knowledge." We then began to press him to define profound knowledge, and he finally did, reluctantly, in 1988. That's when we began to understand the importance of systems, of seeing things in a larger context. As an example, one of the rare defining moments in modern life was when people could see earth from a space capsule, to see for the first time our planet as a pretty little blue and white orb in the universe. Understanding that we are not by ourselves, that we are part of a large, complex system is a big step toward understanding the Deming philosophy.

Things that still interest us—all the "why" questions; that is, we know what he did, but why did he do it?—Deming couldn't answer because he didn't know any better than we did. We think what he became, his interests, and his values grew from his family and the western frontier of his boyhood. This may be the worst kind of cocktail-party pop psychology, but it's hard to understand the man and what he did without seeing him against the background of his childhood. For instance, why would Deming—or anyone, for that matter—celebrate his ninety-third birthday teaching a seminar? Deming did, and even using an oxygen tank and in a wheelchair, he could see no reason why he should not. He died of cancer not quite ten weeks later.

William Edwards Deming was born at 121 Bluff Street in Sioux City, Iowa, the first child of William Albert Deming and Pluma Irene Edwards Deming. Brother Robert was born in May 1902, and the family moved to the boys' maternal grandfather's farm near Polk City, Iowa, two years later. Apparently, the father wanted something better, or different, or his own. The family moved to Cody, Wyoming, when Deming was seven. Deming guessed that his father was drawn westward by free land that could be claimed if they settled there. Deming always added, "Free it was, but with a price of hardship unforeseen." In 1909, the family went twenty-two miles south to Camp Coulter, later renamed Powell, and moved into a tarpaper railroad shack. Sister Elizabeth was born there that year. Deming told us about kneeling with his mother and brother, holding hands, and praying for food to eat as snow blew through the cracks in the tarpaper walls.

Deming's father seems to have been a man of remarkable and wide intelligence, interested in learning for learning's sake, but unable to use any of what he learned to make a steady living. Deming remembered in vivid detail standing in his yard in 1910 looking up at Halley's comet as his father explained the solar system to him. However, asked what his father did, how he supported the family, Deming talked about his father's intelligence, then mentioned a few odd jobs that, listed on a résumé, would not impress anyone. Deming's mother, whom he clearly adored, gave music lessons—piano and voice—and Deming himself went to work when he was about ten; he didn't remember precisely. He did remember that he made $1.25 a week, but, as he reminded you, "Those were gold dollars." The money that Deming made, he said, was sometimes the only money the family had, and he worked his way through the University of Wyoming at Laramie. He could recite every job he had in college and how much he was paid to do it. The worst was outside in winter sawing railroad ties into firewood for two cents a cut.

Money seemed not to mean much to him after his success. He lived in the same modest home he bought in 1936 and owned an eighteen-year-old car. Our guess is that he was at least comfortable monetarily, and he may have been wealthy, but he continued to live and work as he always had. We don't believe he knew how to not work. Teaching and learning were all he wanted to do; they were his work and his fun. His happiest moments seem to have been when he learned seomthing new or made some new connection between data or ideas. He would laugh out loud. After years of being with him, talking to him, and reading his private papers, we can identify only three things other than work that he seemed to enjoy—musical composition, church, and food. In thirteen years, neither of us heard him use the word "vacation."

Like his contemporary the Ayatollah Khomeini, Deming was a zealot with a singular, all-consuming passion. Khomeini wanted to take Iran back to a religious fundamentalism that denied the modern world. Deming wanted to take that modern world forward and make it better for us all. It sounds simplistic, even childish, but that is the aim of the revolution he started—to make life better for us all.

Contents

· · · · ·

Introduction

I have been poor, and I have been rich.
Rich is better.
—*Sophie Tucker*

This is a business book, but it isn't only about business. Many, perhaps most, of the problems faced by the economy today cannot be solved by business alone, no matter how well run and productive each business might become. Businesses, for instance, cannot create high schools that produce educated graduates, nor can they hold down health-care costs that could bankrupt them. Yet businesses, schools, health care, even government services can all be helped by the quality management system advocated by Dr. W. Edwards Deming, a quality philosopher who first became known for helping the Japanese change their industrial management methods after World War II. No one can deny how well that has paid off, not only for the Japanese, but for their customers as well.

What the Japanese learned from Deming and others has already helped a few Americans and Europeans. Employees at the Honda plant in Marysville, Ohio—Americans—told a consultant that they'd rather work at Honda than at an American-run firm because they are treated with greater dignity and respect by the Japanese company. In England, the Industrial Society reports that workers were absent from British-run companies about

5 percent of working hours in 1992, which cost their companies $13 billion. By contrast, British workers in Japanese-managed plants were absent only 3 percent of working hours. That 40 percent saving in costs was a direct bottom-line profit with absolutely no added expense. We don't have comparative figures for the United States, but one report says that for all American business, average absentee rates in 1992 may have been 5 percent and cost $40 billion. Reduce the absentee rate to 3 percent, as Japanese-managed British firms have done, and save $16 billion in one move.

Quality is about profit and satisfaction. This book is not a plea to do good, whatever "good" might mean; it is a plea to make money and stay in business, create new and more interesting jobs, develop new and better products and services, educate more kids, prevent more crime, care for more sick people at less cost—you name it. You can do all those things with the Deming management system, but it isn't easy. Success rarely is, and we have grown extremely leery of anyone who promises enormous quality improvements without effort or change. Years of reporting have made us aware that all con games work on the simple principle that the pigeon thinks he is going to make a huge profit for doing nothing, and while nothing is being done, the pigeon gets plucked. In making the change to a quality system, if a consultant promises that it won't hurt, we promise that it won't help, and it could be enormously expensive. More than one horror story exists about "seagull consultants" who fly in, dump all over you, fly away with your money, and leave you to clean up the mess.*

◆　◆　◆　◆　◆　◆　◆　◆　◆　◆

* We stole the description from Ronald D. Schmidt. You'll meet him later.

We are in favor of anything that makes people aware of the importance of quality to the economic and social health of the nation. That was the reason for our first book, *Quality or Else*, and it is the reason for this one. As reporters, we stumbled on the subject of quality quite by chance while doing research for the 1980 documentary *If Japan Can . . . Why Can't We?* We have learned a lot since then, but not nearly enough. We're still learning, mainly as students and former colleagues of Deming, who was featured in that program. We stayed with the subject of quality because we thought it was a good story, and good stories tend to be too compelling to forget.

We are convinced that unless American managers at all levels adopt quality methods in businesses and public services—education and health care particularly—our children and their children will not live *as well* as our generation is living. Until now, most American children had a good chance of living *better* than their parents did. That comes up a couple of times in the book because it is important to us. We have children, and we don't want to be part of the generation that manages to end more than two hundred years of American growth and expanding prosperity. We don't want to leave our progeny with corporations that can't compete in the world market, schools that don't educate, inadequate and expensive health care, and a national debt so huge the human mind cannot conceive its size. Who can comprehend a trillion dollars? How about three or four trillion? America goes more deeply into debt every second, and whatever you may have been told, nothing of any significance is being done about it. Americans must either change or watch the nation sink.

Just as steam power changed the world forever, quality is changing the world; as the Industrial Revolution created richer and poorer nations, so will the Quality Revolution, and the old rich won't necessarily be the new rich, which is scary if you believe that Sophie Tucker got it right. There are already economists and historians who say, in essence, that just as the other great nations eventually sank, now it is our turn to sink. Believers in economic predestination say it took the Chinese five thousand years to collapse, but the British got it done in a hundred years, and the United States may set a new speed record for collapse. That could be, but it seems timorous at best to willingly sink into second-rate status without even *trying* to stay on top. We think quality could keep us there. That's what this book is about—trying to stay on top.

Chapter 1 is about the mental attitudes and beliefs we all hold that will have to change. These are the attitudes we have observed in traveling around the country talking to others about quality and listening to the objections people raise. We suspect that this is not a complete list, and we'll be happy to receive suggestions, but it's what we've seen often enough to make us think the attitudes we list are widespread. Americans believe too many things that are no longer true, if, indeed, they ever were. That raises the question of what new beliefs will have to replace the old ones and why. We expect that you will argue with some of them, maybe even all of them, and that's fine. Neither one of us has a praiseworthy record in the blind faith department, and we certainly don't expect you to accept anything we say just because we say it. However, if you disagree, you have to say why. Announcing that we are wrong isn't enough. Why are we wrong? More importantly, why are you right? If you say, "Because it's always been that way," you lose.

In chapters 2, 3, and 4 we talk about the philosophy of Deming, the single management system we believe has the best possibility of producing wide-ranging, long-term economic and social results. Chapter 2 is about systems; chapter 3 covers variation, knowledge, and psychology. The two chapters together explain what Deming calls Profound Knowledge. Chapter 4 details the 14 Points* that are a key to the Deming method. We might just as well warn you: we think this is important, perhaps even interesting, but we cannot even pretend that it is entertaining. Subjects called Profound Knowledge and the 14 Points don't quicken the pulse. We are certain, however, that until you are acquainted with that much of Deming's philosophy, you have little or no hope of understanding what it is doing or why it is doing it, or how your organization might improve.

In chapter 5, we show how the material from chapters 2, 3, and 4 was applied by Zytec, a midwestern electronics company, and applied so successfully that the improvements it achieved sound too good to be true. Seven years after the company started using the Deming quality management system, it won the Malcolm Baldrige National Quality Award. On the other hand, the Wallace Company, of Texas also won the Baldrige Award and fifteen months later filed for bankruptcy protection. We explain what we think the difference between the two companies was. Why did one company win and prosper

♦   ♦   ♦   ♦   ♦   ♦   ♦   ♦   ♦   ♦

* The 14 Points have nothing to do with the similarly named World War I peace program proposed by President Woodrow Wilson in 1918 when Deming was a freshman at the University of Wyoming in Laramie.

and the other win and go belly up? We can't prove our analysis is correct, but it's the only explanation that we believe covers all the facts.

In chapter 6, we compare Deming's 14 Points and the seven criteria by which Baldrige contestants are judged. Deming didn't like Baldrige, but Zytec used his philosophy and his 14 Points to win the award, and we try to show how that can be done.

Congress created the Malcolm Baldrige National Quality Award in 1987 (chapter 7), the first concrete step ever taken by the United States government to improve productivity nationally. The award represents the ideas of a number of quality experts, and the criteria for the prize are praised as the first compendium of almost everything known or believed about quality methods. Originally, we had intended this book to be more about the Baldrige Award and less about the Deming method, but the more we tried to explain Baldrige, the more we wrote about Deming. Their roles in the book were getting reversed, so we gave up and did what we should have done in the first place—show you how the Deming method produces quality, and how quality produces the Baldrige Award.

The Baldrige Award is the best-known American prize for quality, and its importance is growing. Former congressman Don Ritter, a Pennsylvania Republican, predicts that someday it will "rival the Nobel Prize in capturing the imagination of the American people." Whether his prediction turns out to be true or not, the Baldrige Award could be and should be better. That is not much of a criticism since it can be said of almost everything. George Murray, a director with a television network news team at the Vatican in 1978, was asked by a colleague what he thought on first seeing Michelangelo's ceiling in the

Sistine Chapel. "It's nice," he said, staring up at it, "but I'd have done it differently."

Chapter 8 explains how George Westinghouse Vocational and Technical High School is doing it differently, providing a quality education for inner-city youths, 99 percent of whom are members of racial minorities. Westinghouse does not use a strict Deming quality system, but it is basically Deming, and it works in a school where every single social indicator says the system and the students should fail. We also do a little reporting on quality in health care to demonstrate that it works just as well in that area as it does everywhere else.

Chapter 9 discusses how the Deming quality management system works in the Department of the Navy, where, by the way, the old Total Quality Control program was renamed Total Quality Management. Now you know how that name, inevitably abbreviated TQM, came about. The Navy program is now called Total Quality Leadership to emphasize who is responsible for it. We also mention the program under way at the *New York Times* on the business side. The editorial people—those who write and edit the paper—do not appear to be completely convinced yet that it would work for them.

In the final chapter, we consider government and its role in quality, but we also tie up loose ends, mention some bits and pieces that we find interesting, and suggest some questions for which we have no answers, just speculation and guesses. For instance, we think there is a connection between ethical organizational behavior and quality management—which we find fascinating—but we can't prove it.

Two things we need to explain to prevent possible confusion:

The Deming method requires *continual* improvement. Most Americans speak of *"continuous* improvement," and when that is what was said, that is what we quoted. However, the two words are not true synonyms, and Deming insisted on the distinction. *Continuous* means "unbroken, never-ending"; *continual* means "occurring on a frequent or regular basis." Think of trying to read this book to the end: You may face continual interruptions, but you will eventually finish it. If you have a continuous interruption, you'll never get back to the book. Or anything else.

We mention several times that "mission, vision, and guiding principles" are absolutely essential, but the Ford Motor Company started with "mission, values, and guiding principles." You can argue that vision is implicit in mission or that values are implicit in guiding principles. The people at Ford decided one way; we decided the other. It's not important so long as you understand that you must know where you are going, why, and what you believe.

There are other definitions you need to know, but they are in the chapters where you'll need them. They help you understand what a quality management system is, even though none of the experts totally agree on what the word "quality" means.

In the nation whose citizens had developed, then perfected, mass production, quality before 1980 was almost as important a national priority as dessert forks at a pig pickin'. The president of an American television-manufacturing company once said that there was no reason to make a television set any better than what was minimally required to sell it. In those days of planned obsolescence, his comment shocked no one; it was received economic wisdom. That attitude is now disappearing in American industry, but not before most of the jobs in the American consumer electronics industry have been lost to foreign manufacturers who want their customers not only to buy the product but to be delighted with it. The Malcolm Baldrige National Quality Award was the result of a growing, often reluctant, recognition in America that the world had changed.

Quality has replaced quantity in the world market, and American companies must adapt. American managers have to replace traditional, or quantity, management with quality management. If managers everywhere—in government, schools, hospitals, law enforcement—would adopt quality management systems, we'd get improvements in problem areas that we now don't even recognize as being related. Only a handful of people have noticed that many of our problems grow from the same basic cause—we manage poorly. They are not likely to notice until they become more aware of and concerned with quality.

We hope this book will help make more people aware that American management in all fields must shift from quantity to quality. Many American businesses and industrial leaders have already shifted or are shifting. We are less certain that leaders in government and social areas understand the implications of quality systems to their own management.

Americans have been raised to believe in the separation of business and government and education and health care and everything else. Americans like each thing in its own neat pigeonhole, but as we have progressed and our organizations have grown more complex, we have become more interdependent, and the pigeonholes that used to keep everything tidy now make it harder to see how interrelated they are. At least one critic has said that quality management systems cannot be the solution to everything. Why not? Since the days of the Industrial Revolution, we have used quantity management systems to run everything. Except for a few institutions that have had the courage to change, our schools and hospitals are being run exactly as are our factories and stores.

The problem is not that each field needs some special management system; the problem is that all fields need a better system. All we need to do is replace the quantity management system we have used in this century with Deming's quality management system that we will need in the future. It will work perfectly well—everywhere.

As we said at the beginning, this is a business book, but it's about everybody's business.

Lloyd Dobyns
Garner, North Carolina

Clare Crawford-Mason
Washington, D.C.

January 1994

Thinking About Quality

· · · ·

1

· · · · ·

The Devils

The will to believe is perhaps the most powerful,
but certainly the most dangerous human attribute.
—*John P. Grier*

The best way to make people understand that there is a basic problem with the economy of the United States is to state the problem bluntly: American managers, by and large, don't know how to manage; not just in manufacturing, but in the service industry, in education, in health care, and in government at all levels. That is not because American managers are stupid, but because they are smart. They were taught how to manage in school and by experience, they learned it better than anyone else in the world, and they don't want to give it up. They were taught; they learned; they are comfortable.

What they were taught, what they learned, what they are comfortable with doesn't work. It used to, but it doesn't anymore.

That's hardly shocking. What we were all taught over the last fifty years in all fields is changing so rapidly that it defies our ability to adapt. It's easier to accept the changes in technology because you can see the advantages. In writing, for instance, when you compare manual typewriters with word processors, no one can miss the vast improvement. Because of the obvious, enormous, and immediate benefit, people go through the frustration and bother of changing and of learning new skills, even if they wish they didn't have to. They can *see* the need.

The concept of quality management, developed since World War II, does not involve technology; it involves thought. You have to stop thinking about quantity and start thinking about quality. What makes that more difficult is that quality isn't a convenient list you can consult or even anything you can look at. Thinking is an invisible process, and what American managers must change if we are to survive is how they think and what they believe. The world is developing a new economic game, and the players who appear to do best are those who know how to think *quality* methods. American managers have been taught to think *quantity*. That has to change, but only a fool or a masochist thinks change is easy or fun.

Years of experience demonstrate that persuading people to change to quality methods is not a matter of marshaled fact and cogent argument. Change is so difficult that people must *believe* it is necessary. Executives generally turn to quality only when they believe that if they continue to do what they've been doing their companies will not survive. They may not be in trouble at that moment—most aren't—but smart executives can look toward the future and see trouble coming if they don't change. Once they *believe* survival is at stake, recommending that they adopt a quality management system is simpler.

Getting them to change from the old quantity belief to the new quality belief is the hard and important part, because belief beats facts hands down. If people operated on a factual basis, everyone would have adopted a quality method by now. The fact is that quality methods provide better results. Another fact is that people who work in quality companies are happier, better-trained, and more dedicated employees. An even bigger fact is that quality is the standard of competition in the global market.

Those facts don't win converts because people don't operate factually. They operate emotionally, and emotion is controlled by belief. The accepted estimate is that only 10 to 40 percent of the information each of us carries around mentally is fact. All the rest of what is in our minds—up to 90 percent—is belief or misinformation we've picked up from popular myths or outdated teaching. Once those erroneous beliefs are in our heads, getting them out is always tough, and occasionally impossible. People deeply resent being told that part of what they believe is wrong. Just as perception is reality, belief is truth—and powerful truth. All the world's religions are based on belief.

Some of our everyday beliefs get between us and quality methods because we never learned, or have forgotten, the advice of Harold Geneen, former chairman of ITT: "We must not be hampered by yesterday's myths in concentrating on today's needs." We *are* hampered. Americans can't accept that quality methods work; too many of the quality requirements disagree with what we as a people have long believed to be true. Only a relatively few people *oppose* quality methods. Most who resist are only clinging to what they believe, unable or unwilling to change no matter what the facts may be. That mind-load of beliefs and myths, many so deeply ingrained we aren't even aware we have them, bogs us in a mire of immobility. We have those beliefs reinforced all the time.*

During the 1992 presidential campaign, on a network evening newscast, then President George Bush said, "Competition never hurt anything." He meant it, and we suspect that the vast majority of Americans who heard the broadcast agreed with him or at least accepted his statement as wisdom. Accepted or not, it's wrong. In his book *No Contest: The Case Against Competition*, Alfie Kohn identifies and debunks the competitive myths we so easily accept. We compete and are taught to compete from our earliest days, and we believe that we *must* compete to succeed. We are told that competition is part of human nature, that it brings out the best in us, that it's fun (for the winners), and that competition builds character (for the losers). None of that is true. Dr. W. Edwards Deming, the quality philosopher, said, "Competition is our ruination."

We are talking about competition within a company or an organization or competition among groups of people who ought to be working together—division heads of corporations, students, team members. Anywhere there should be teamwork and cooperation, there must *not* be competition. What Mr. Bush should have said—although only a handful of Americans would have believed him— was, "*Cooperation* never hurt anything." In any quality program, cooperation is a requirement. "What we need to

◆　◆　◆　◆　◆　◆　◆　◆　◆　◆

* Comparing what we used to believe with what we need to believe was suggested by Robert W. Mason. In a speech in October 1992, he compared what he had been taught and believed as a Harvard MBA with what he believes now. (It's okay if I borrow the idea; we're married. [C.C.-M.])

do," Deming said, "is learn to work in the system, by which I mean that everybody, every team, every platform, every division, every component is there not for individual competitive profit or recognition, but for contribution to the system as a whole on a win-win basis."

Cooperation is always productive; conflict, defined as "a state of open, often prolonged fighting" never is; and competition may be productive if it is a conflict with rules and a cooperative aim. Most of what people call competition is really conflict—the sole object of the exercise is to destroy the opponent. In competition, as Dr. Russell L. Ackoff, a systems sciences educator and consultant, points out, there may well be a cooperative purpose. He uses the example of a tennis game. It is a conflict because one player will win, the other will lose. It is also cooperation because both players have agreed to play by the same rules. While one player wins and one player loses, that is not the only, and often not even the more important, aim. Another aim, among amateurs at least, is to enjoy the contest, get some exercise perhaps, and have fun. If the conflict is uneven—one player is clearly superior—then the purpose of "having fun" is destroyed for both players. To have fun, it must be an equal competition played under agreed rules.

The same circumstances can be applied in business. "It's perfectly okay," Ackoff says, "to have parts of organizations compete with one another, providing that their conflict is serving the purpose of the whole more effectively than they could otherwise." As an example, neither tennis player could have as much fun, get as much exercise, or be as challenged by hitting a ball off a wall. What gives the game value is the cooperative competition.

If you want a clear example of the power of conflict

(called competition) to do harm, you need to look no further than the competition among the states to lure business and industry. In the process, states give free land, low-interest loans, and billions of dollars' worth of tax breaks. Industry plays the states against each other, fishing for higher subsidies with new jobs as bait. One state will win; all others will lose. No higher purpose is served; there are no agreed rules; there is no cooperation. When states are already getting to be almost as short of cash as the federal government, "buying" industrial development makes no sense, particularly when the "sale" doesn't go through. North Carolina gave financial incentives to RJR Nabisco to get it to build a huge new bakery near Garner, southeast of Raleigh. When the largest leveraged buyout in corporate history left RJR Nabisco up to its chocolate chips in debt, the new bakery was "postponed" into the next century. Even if the bakery is built some time in the distant future, North Carolina may never recover all the money it used to "buy" the bakery, because the tax breaks for RJR Nabisco also applied to other firms and, according to one report, North Carolina loses $30 million a year in taxes.

If the states would cooperate, refuse to compete, all business and industry would still have to locate somewhere and pay taxes that would help states improve their education, health care, and law enforcement to the benefit of everyone in the area, including the new industries. That isn't likely to happen in today's competitive world. A newspaper article reports, "[Governor Jim] Hunt says that other states are handing out wads of cash and that if North Carolina wants to remain in the game, it's got to ante up." He is also quoted as assuring taxpayers that there will not be another "RJR fiasco." Perhaps not in North

Carolina, but as long as the states continue to compete for industry, there will be another fiasco somewhere.

Another place where the price of competition is obvious and painful is the Congress of the United States. The country is now deeply in debt and saddled with social problems that are so horrendous they defy description. Members of Congress have not been able to help solve those problems as well as they should have because they are organized to compete, not to cooperate. The members are elected in their districts or states to represent those districts and states, and meeting those local needs is the only way to win reelection. Representative David E. Price (D-N.C.) says he spends as much time in his district as he does in Washington, and we doubt he is unique.

Even though all members talk about national policy and national needs, the truth is that no member of Congress is elected to represent the nation. Speeches on national subjects may get all sorts of media coverage, but national issues don't win reelection campaigns. What does win is "pork," federal money for projects at home, and what that spending might do to the nation's budget or its debt or its economic future is not a consideration. Senator Alfonse D'Amato (R-N.Y.) talks often of the need to cut government spending—space and agriculture are targets— but he has been so successful at getting federal highway funds for New York, he's nicknamed "Senator Pothole." We don't mention that as a criticism. He was elected to take care of New York in a competition with other states, and he's good at it. He's not nearly as good as Senator Robert Byrd (D-W.Va.), whose ability to "pork" the budget borders on the legendary. Humorist Dave Barry now identifies Byrd's affiliation not as "(D-W.Va.)," but as "(D-Pork)." Neither Byrd nor D'Amato was elected to take care of the nation, but we are certain that each would deeply resent any implication that his actions were harmful to the nation.

Depending on how well the two senators from each state get along, the Senate is, for any practical purpose, fifty to a hundred divisions of a huge corporation, each trying to outdo the others, and no one of them is more concerned about the health of the corporation (nation) as a whole than about the well-being of his or her division (state). There is no incentive to cooperate among the senators—other than trading votes for often suspect projects—and the result is that billions of dollars have been haphazardly thrown at problems or pet projects, not necessarily to solve anything, but to attract votes. That is not because senators are villains but because that is how the U.S. Senate is organized.

According to the accepted myths, congressional competition should have brought out the best in our representatives and senators, should have been a lot of fun for them, and should have built their characters. It has done none of that, and the only thing that has been built is debt, not character. The United States is so far in the hole that we may one day be forced to rely on the equally absurd myth from the Great Depression that poverty builds character.

Members of Congress should be cooperating to make the United States better able to compete in the global market. Instead, they compete with one another for their districts and states, and the nation is *less* able to compete. The same sort of competitive harm is done inside companies, schools, hospitals, and other levels of government. We are so busy competing with each other that we are harming our own ability to compete as a country in the global market. Inside a company, the idea that competition makes us better leads to personnel systems that rank and rate employees against each other. How can anyone work cooperatively as part of a team when that cooperation might help another worker get a higher personnel rating, perhaps even a merit pay increase? The old idea that competition (conflict) leads to the best work is wrong. Cooperation does.

The paradox is that we must cooperate to become better able to compete.

There is one area of competition that is natural, brings out the best, is fun, and builds character. That is our competition with ourselves. We compete internally to improve, to get a bit smarter or better at what we do; and for each of us to be better does not require that the rest of us, or even one of us, be worse. That is the old win-lose thinking, but with cooperation, we all can win. We cooperate with others and compete with ourselves as individuals. Companies cooperate and compete: Motorola has a joint venture with a Japanese manufacturer with which it also competes. We compete as countries in the global market while we cooperate to keep the peace, increase trade, and help developing countries. That balance of cooperation and competition produces winners everywhere who enjoy better products at less cost using fewer of the world's diminishing natural resources.

That is the first of the old beliefs that needs to change. To make it easier for you to follow, here's a list of the fifteen devils, obstacles to the acceptance of the new quality management philosophy.

◆ ◆ ◆   ◆ ◆ ◆

Old	**New**
Competition motivates people to do better work.	Cooperation helps people do more effective work.
For every winner there's a loser.	Everyone can win.
Please your boss.	Please your customer.
Scapegoating pinpoints problems.	Improve the system.
Focus improvement on individual processes.	Focus on the purpose of the overall system, and how the processes can be improved to serve it better.
Find the cause and fix the problem.	First, acknowledge there is variation in all things and people. See if the problem falls in or outside the system.
The job is complete if specifications have been met.	Continual improvement is an unending journey.
Inspection and measurement ensure quality.	A capable process, shared vision and aim, good leadership and training are major factors in creating quality.

Old	**New**
Risks and mistakes are bad.	Risks are necessary and some mistakes inevitable when you practice continual improvement.
You can complete your education.	Everyone is a lifelong learner.
Bosses command and control.	Bosses help workers learn and make improvements.
Bosses have to know everything.	The team with a good leader knows and can do more.
Short-term payoffs are best.	Significant achievement in a complex world takes time.
You don't have to be aware of your basic beliefs.	You must be conscious of your beliefs and constantly examine and test them to see if they continue to be true.
Do it now.	Think first, then act.

◆ ◆ ◆ ◆ ◆

Just as we must change what we do, we must change why we do it. Employees have long believed that the way to get ahead is to please the boss. Since early in the twentieth century, when mass production began, pleasing the boss *was* the way to get ahead. It no longer is. With quality, the customer rules, so you and your boss have to work together to please the customer. That stands the normal organizational chart on its head. The customer at the bottom (if he's on the chart at all) and the CEO on top trade places. "As an employee," says consultant Peter Scholtes, "it's important for you *not* to please your boss; it's important for you to please your customer. That change requires a profound change of mind in our organizations. Very, very difficult." And dangerous, as Scholtes points out. You can't make this decision on your own. It's critical that your boss understand and agree with your shift in focus from boss to customer. William Congreve, the English dramatist who wrote of the fury of a woman scorned, never observed the rage of a modern American executive ignored. Adding yourself to the ranks of the unemployed is not helpful.

The definition of customer expands in most quality programs to include internal and external customers.* The external customer is fairly obvious: it's whoever is paying the bill for the product. The internal customer is whoever depends on your work. On an assembly line or in the accounting department, it is whoever works next on what you have done, or, to put it another way, the internal customer is the person who relies on your having done it right. "The idea," Dr. Myron Tribus, a consultant, says, "is that you organize the work of people so that each person

• • • • • • • • • •

* There are several recognized quality programs. We discussed them in chapters 3 and 4 of *Quality or Else.*

tries to please the next person in line, treat the next person in line as a customer."

However you define "customer," that customer is the person who will define "quality" for you. The generally accepted definition is that, with some specific limitations, quality is whatever the customer says it is. That grew out of a sentence the author Robert Pirsig wrote nearly twenty years ago: "Even though quality cannot be defined, *you know what quality is.*" By the 1980s that definition had companies talking about the need for customer satisfaction, which turns out to be not enough. Howard Wilson, the director of market-driven quality in corporate services at IBM, explained that to us several years ago. Essentially, he said, if you don't satisfy the customer, the customer sooner or later will find someone who does. If you do satisfy the customer, he or she may come back or may give someone else a try. If you want the customer to return, then that customer must be delighted. The way to delight customers is to give them something that they did not expect. Wilson calls this the delight factor.

In a radio commercial for TWA that was on the air in April 1993, an airline customer described the additional leg room in TWA's coach class as "a prize, something you didn't expect for the same amount of money." Delight factor. It doesn't have to be expensive. Ask around and at least one answer is that an important delight factor in the hotel business is not the minibar in the room, or the free toiletries, or the wrapped chocolate on the pillow, but being called by name by the desk clerks. It makes sense. As we become part of an ever-more high-tech society, each of us seems to have a growing need to be reminded that he or she is something more than the sum of a Social Security number.

The traditional American management system does recognize individuals, but in a way we could all do without. One of our most enduring beliefs is that if anything goes wrong, someone—some single solitary soul—must be responsible for it. The way to solve that problem, therefore, is to find that someone and, as a corporate acquaintance of ours phrased it, "make the guilty bastard pay!" It is the accepted, time-honored solution, and the only thing wrong with it is that it doesn't work. The belief in the value of a scapegoat comes from the Bible, and the explanation is in Leviticus, starting at 16:21. The children of Israel are instructed to symbolically put the sins and iniquities of the tribe on the head of a goat each year and drive that goat into the wilderness, casting out their own wrongdoing. The Israelites are not told to send each other into the wilderness to die for their inadequacies. The symbol goes; the people stay. (A friend asked, "Does the goat get to 'scape into the desert?" Yes, we know, but we take humor where we find it.)

Another change we haven't made is best understood from the *I Ching*, a book of Chinese poems and text that may date to the second millennium B.C. and probably was written as we know it by the seventh century B.C. Also known as *The Book of Changes*, it's a favorite of fortune-tellers today, but it was used much earlier to develop a theory of the universe. Confucius drew on it to suggest that learning could lead anyone to find a proper place in the moral cosmos. The book describes a fluid world of continuous beginnings and endings and describes a way to turn crisis to opportunity. The *I Ching* is, in other words, concerned with systems. Dr. Russell L. Ackoff says that interest in systems has been dominant in Eastern thinking for thousands of years, but doesn't show up in Western thinking until the 1930s in Germany.

"The systems revolution," he says, "involves two things: It involves the concept of a system, and it involves the use of science. We had science, but not the concept of a system. [Asians] had the concept of a system, but not the concept of science." That prevailed until after World War II. "What's been happening," Ackoff says, "is [Asians] have been absorbing the concept of science faster than [Westerners] have been absorbing the concept of a system." Our ability to understand systems, the new requirement, is hampered by our inability to accept that the system itself, not some person or process in it, is to blame for what goes wrong.

The reason that is important is that quality methods generally teach that everything is a system, and that to improve quality, you must improve the system as a whole. As a rule, unless there is a willful rebellion under way, you can't find who is to blame when something goes wrong, and too rarely to mention can anyone in a system produce more than the system is organized to produce. Blaming or rewarding individuals for what the system does is fruitless at best and usually harmful. You don't know who, if anyone, deserves a bonus, and you can't tell who, if anyone, should be the scapegoat. Looking for that scapegoat does nothing to fix the system that allowed the mistake to occur, and if you are looking for *someone* to blame, you cannot be looking for the *something* that went wrong in the system, which could mean that at some point in the future it may go wrong again. And to make your life truly miserable, even that is not guaranteed.

Americans have lived this century with the certainty

of cause and effect—if we did this, that would happen. We are only now beginning to come to terms with variation, a statistical concept that goes well past mathematics into how we learn and live. The Deming management system teaches that variation exists in all things and in all people, and unless you understand and plan for that variation, you can—and probably will—make a major mess. By studying variation, you can see whether a mistake is built into the system and likely will recur or whether a mistake is straight out of the blue, an often unexplainable glitch that may never happen again. If you don't understand the theory of variation, you will try to fix an unexplainable glitch, which can't be done and will cost a lot to look for; or you will try to ignore a glitch built into the system, which can't be done and will cost a lot as it continually recurs. The old requirement was to find the cause and fix the problem no matter what. The new requirement is to decide if the mistake is in the system and has to be fixed or is outside the system and can be ignored. For the American manager trained in traditional cause and effect, it is all but impossible to accept that there is a mistake that may not be worth trying to find and fix. That mistake could be an effect with no known cause, a concept we have been trained to resist.

It is that sort of nondefinitive thinking that is difficult to accept, just as it is difficult to accept that some efforts will never be finished. A quality method requires continual improvement because, hard as it is to accept, no process or product (or person) ever gets to be perfect. Continual improvement through quality methods is, therefore, the antithesis of the conventional wisdom "If it ain't broke, don't fix it." As Peter Scholtes says, that often-quoted bromide "has a facile, surface logic." It sounds right, and before we had quality methods, it probably was good advice. If you didn't understand what your system was doing anyway, trying to make the system better could accidentally actually make it better. Of course, it could just as easily make it worse. That sort of fiddling around for the fun of it is known in quality methods as tampering, and all the experts are opposed to it. Now that we know how systems work, the goal is continual improvement, and waiting for something to break is a mistake. Besides, how do you know you can fix it if it does break?

We suggest that public education in the United States has been broken at least since World War II, and every attempt to fix it has (a) cost a ton and (b) made it worse. Wouldn't the country and its youngsters be better off if we had continually improved public education using quality methods instead of waiting for it to break down? Where quality methods have been used in education, the success has been remarkable. Most educators are as tied to the traditional management system as are most industrialists, and the two groups are equally reluctant to embrace a new method. They cling to their beliefs and ask for more money to try some new experiment in the same old system.

Public officials demand tighter standards and call for achievement tests to be certain that high school graduates have certain minimum acceptable skills. Tests are like inspections; they're designed to discover what's been done wrong, but they don't tell you how to improve the system that produced uneducated high school seniors in the first place. Inspection does not create quality; tests cannot create education. They can confirm that a problem exists, but we already know that a problem exists; confirmation isn't necessary or even desirable. The old belief was that inspection produced quality. What is necessary in the new economy is continual improvement to eliminate the current problem and prevent future problems, even when we don't know what those future problems might be.

It isn't a matter of finish by Friday and get a good grade; it's a matter of always getting better, experimenting, and being willing to fail. "He who has never failed somewhere," Herman Melville wrote, "that man can not be great." In the American management system, failure at some project has always been ink spilled on your career copybook, usually a guarantee that the next promotion has just slipped far into the future, so far, perhaps, that it never comes. In the old management method, risks and even minor failures were things to be avoided at all costs. In the modern world, risk is a requirement. (Don't get carried away: There is a difference between instructive failure, where calculated risks teach what not to do, and old-fashioned, boneheaded incompetence.) In the global economy, where everything moves faster than it ever has before, where every new technology can be outdated tomorrow, companies not willing for their people to take calculated risks, some of which are bound to fail, will usually be a couple of steps behind. Being late to the market could destroy the company. Whoever gets to the market with a new product first almost always profits most. In competition, as in comedy, timing counts.

What is most important is that we Americans must learn to think in a new way about ourselves, a way that is not particularly flattering at first, but that works out rather well. We must accept that we aren't nearly as smart as we think we are, that a college degree, even an advanced degree, does not mean that we are educated. There was a time when knowledge didn't change that quickly, but that was a long time ago, back when students were still being taught that the atom was the smallest unit of matter and could not be split. In those days, a college education was for a lifetime.

In a global economy, education is much like quality; it's a matter of continual improvement throughout life. We aren't doing that yet. In a society in which 20 percent of the adult population have college degrees, less than 10 percent in any year read a book more difficult than popular fiction. Some estimates are even lower than that, but that is low enough to make the point: American colleges and universities have handed degrees to about twice as many people as they have educated. The old idea that education was something that could be completed has to give way to the modern requirement for lifelong learning. Society would be better served if every degree from every institution had stamped across its face in two-inch-high red letters "Learner's Permit."

Deming continued until his death to learn and to develop his management system. Central to it are his 14 Points, which he developed in the 1970s out of years of experience trying to teach other people how to achieve quality. Two of the 14 Points require training for job skills and education. Deming was careful to emphasize in his seminars that the two should not be confused. Skills training—those things you need to do your job to the best of your ability—should continue only as long as it takes for each person to learn. Once a painter knows what there is to know about paint flow, brushes, rollers, drip cloths, masking tape, and straight lines, there is no point to continued training. If some new development—say, the spray gun—makes a difference in the industry, then is the time for additional training.

That's an ideal, so far. Most American firms do no training now. Even among major corporations that do train, most of the budget is spent to train managers. That may be changing, particularly among small companies that traditionally said training was too expensive. Early in 1993, one survey found that only 3 to 5 percent of small companies had training programs in place, but another 20 percent wanted to start them. Small-business owners are learning that training can make the difference between success and failure. In most cases, the training is in specific job skills and is for a limited period.

Education is different. Since you can never know everything, education must continue, and it is better, according to Deming, if that education has little or nothing to do with your job. That's the point where traditional American managers balk. Major corporations consider it reasonable to pay for a course in advanced accounting for a new accountant, but even some of the best companies seem reluctant to pay for a course in philosophy or art appreciation or Japanese flower arranging.

Worker education in unrelated areas may have a better payoff in the long run than skills training, but it is, we admit, impossible to measure or prove. The theory is that as a worker is forced to think of a new topic in a new way, he or she will bring that new thinking skill to the job. Thinking of the old job in a new way could create a new solution. For instance, Japanese flower arranging requires the eye of a designer searching for maximum artistic benefit with minimum materials, which is one way to describe creating a better product for less money. Even if there is no breakthrough, the worker will be smarter, and that is an asset. What will provide commercial success in the twenty-first century is a work force of highly educated, highly motivated people.

That causes another change in our beliefs. Self-motivated, highly educated workers do not need supervisors standing over them giving orders. Ever since Frederick W. Taylor published his "scientific" management theory in 1911, factories have been organized so that each individual worker does one tiny task exactly as he is told to do it, and that's that. No deviation, no thinking, no innovation, lots of supervision. If Taylor accomplished nothing else, he created a bonanza for supervisory employment. "Between 1910 and 1920," one report says, "the ranks of supervisory employees grew nearly two and a half times as fast as the ranks of wage earners."

Quality methods require just the opposite—fewer supervisors and the complete involvement of the people doing the work in deciding how that work gets done. That changes the relationship of management and labor. First, less management is needed, which may explain why early in 1993, for the first time since records have been kept, there were more unemployed white-collar workers than blue-collar workers. Second, the management that remains is there to assist the workers, not to give them orders. It is a change that some line managers cannot make, just as some senior managers cannot bring themselves to accept that the success of the company does not rest on how smart they are but on how smart and capable their workers are.

In quantity manufacturing, the boss had to know it all and had to command and control the work force. No more. The boss has to make it possible for the workers to get the job done cooperatively. As many old ideas as we attack, we should recognize those that stand up in the modern world. We are used to saying, "Two heads are better than one." Now we have to mean it.

This involvement of the work force causes some confusion. Even though workers have a voice in how things get done, and middle managers are there to help them do it, we are not describing anarchy, or even democracy. The boss is still the boss, but instead of saying, "No," he or she now says, "No, and here's why." The difference is that the boss now decides only those issues the boss should decide, and leaves the daily bits and pieces that are a natural part of all jobs to the people doing those jobs. That frees the top people to worry about and plan for the future. That is one of the pleasant parts of the Deming method that too few people recognize: It allows every person in an enterprise to concentrate on what that person is supposed to do, knowing that other areas are being handled just as well by other people.

There is another area of change that is going to be difficult, especially for Americans. We are a monumentally impatient people who want everything finished yesterday, and if it can't be done quickly, Americans question whether it is worth doing at all. Quality doesn't work that way. The Deming management system takes years because it is a philosophy, not a technique. Thinking is always more difficult and time-consuming in a quality management system than doing, but if you are impatient for results, being told to "be patient" is infuriating. Americans believe that everything can be done quickly— ipso facto, everything that isn't quick must be bad. That's another myth that has to go.

In a complex organization, significant improvements

are long-term and worth the time and effort it takes to achieve them. Americans have not gotten into the current mess in the last two weeks, and we are not going to get out of it in the next two.

Since the Deming method takes time, in some places it has already become suspect. Some management consultants warn that giving up short-term goals is a bad idea. In 1992 and '93, the *Wall Street Journal, Newsweek,* the *Economist,* the *Washington Post,* and *Inc. Magazine* all had articles declaring quality dead, dying, or outdated. *Inc.* said that the failure of the Wallace Company after winning the Malcolm Baldrige National Quality Award calls into question the value of quality methods, all of which it mistakenly lumps together as Total Quality Management. The article didn't mention the other sixteen companies that have won the Baldrige and appear to be doing rather well. Dr. Curt W. Reimann, director of the Baldrige Award, said in July 1993, "All Award winners have improved productivity on a sustained basis, most quite dramatically."

Baldrige Award winners that are traded on the New York Stock Exchange have been especially good investments. According to *Business Week* magazine, $1,000 invested in the stock of award winners on the days their awards were announced would have shown a gain of 89.2 percent, excluding dividends, by the fall of 1993. The same theoretical investment in shares in an accepted stock index would have grown only 33.1 percent. Not all Baldrige winners have done well, but the good have made much more than the bad have lost. The two winners in 1988 were Westinghouse and Motorola. Westinghouse has lost 47.5 percent of its share price, but Motorola has

gained 442.3 percent. Even with that level of performance, people still remain suspicious of the concept of
quality.

Part of the problem, we think, is that the word "quality" doesn't mean anything concrete, and the word is
sometimes used as a sales gimmick to try to cover up a
complete lack of quality. On a recent television program,
one character asked, "Have you ever noticed when something's not quite up to snuff, they put a word like 'quality'
in front of it?" It isn't always true, but it happens too often
to be ignored.

The TQM du jour is whatever the consultant says it is,
and that concept is so abused by so many people that it
has come to mean nothing at all. In May 1993, a newspaper columnist, in declaring "Japanese management" dead,
identified quality as automation, quality circles, and just-
in-time deliveries; then he carefully explained why they
wouldn't work in the United States. He got that wrong as
well.

What we may need is a new word, something to describe what's going on in the Deming management system
that has an agreed-upon meaning we can all accept.
Pirsig's seminal work, *Zen and the Art of Motorcycle
Maintenance*, has as its subtitle, *An Inquiry into Values.*
Alan Benedict, who studies quality methods, after a personal review of *Lila*, Pirsig's second book, suggests that we
stop saying "quality" altogether because "the more you try
to grasp Quality, the more it slips away. . . . Personally," he
wrote, "I always thought 'value' summed it up pretty well.
I can understand that a Ford Taurus may be a better value
than a Rolls-Royce, but I have a hard time seeing it as having greater quality."

Using the word "value" is not a bad idea. Even with

the outmoded concepts of mass production, you can achieve quality if there are enough inspectors and they are allowed to be rigorous and demanding. You cannot, however, achieve value. Years ago, a magazine ad for a fountain pen touted its quality by bragging about the number of inspections each pen had to pass. The pen had high quality and an equally high price. The Deming method, on the other hand, aims to achieve that extreme level of quality at a *reasonable price*, and that is one meaning of value. If a new word would help people understand what must be done, then we are for a new word. In this book, we'll stick with "quality," but if you like "value" better, it suits us. Whatever word you use, what you are talking about is the *system* by which quality or value or (insert your word here) is produced.

2

• • • • •

Systems

*Discovery consists of seeing what everybody has seen
and thinking what nobody has thought.*
—*Albert Szent-Györgyi*

Since 1775, when James Watt built a working model of
his steam engine, we have lived in the Age of Machines,
and those machines have been particularly good to us.
Without them, we would not live nearly as well as we do.
To continue to live well, however, we have to move beyond the machines to a new age that people can describe,
but not yet name, even though a name would be helpful.
It would help people think about what is happening.

Michael Hammer and James Champy, coauthors of
Reengineering the Corporation, see it as "the postindustrial
business age." That is the description; the name is different: "The curtain is rising on the Age of Reengineering,"
they announce at the end of their book. Reengineering is
what they advocate, but the name only makes sense to the
relatively few who already know what it means.

Peter Drucker, one of the country's leading management thinkers, sees a future in which the knowledgeable
replace capitalists in importance, hence a *Post-Capitalist
Society*, which happens to be the title of his latest book.
We agree on the increasing value of knowledge, but writing off capitalists seems almost as premature as writing off

industry. We don't think industry or capitalists are dead yet.

Walter B. Wriston, former chairman of Citicorp, is quite firm in what he believes the name should be: "It is the Information Age," which is *not* the title of his book. We admit that his candidate is a popular name, but information is only a bunch of random facts. It is what you *do* with the information that matters.

We can agree on names we don't like, but we have been unable to agree between the two of us on a name that is completely accurate, clearly descriptive, and catchy. Obviously, if we had agreed, it would be the title of this book. *Thinking About Quality* may be accurate and descriptive, but it fails the catchy test hands down. Since we have to call this period of time something, we call it the Age of Continual Improvement. It, too, is a flop catchy-wise, as they say in ad circles. We doubt that anyone will be moved to write a toe-tapping tune in celebration, but it is accurate and descriptive, or reasonably so. We don't expect it to catch on.

What you call the new society or precisely how you describe its details is not as important as recognizing that what we have known and done in the past is not what we will have to know and do in the future. Just as we must change the myths and misinformation that we have believed, we also must change how we think about what we do. To put it another way: Whoever said this was going to be easy?

In *Post-Capitalist Society*, Drucker argues that in the future, knowledge and organization are going to be much more closely related than they are now. The knowledgeable person—essential to our future—will have to be comfortable in both worlds, "that of the 'intellectual,' who focuses on words and ideas," he writes, "and that of the 'manager,' who focuses on people and work."

After visiting hundreds of factories, schools, hospitals, and government agencies in the United States, Europe, and Asia, after talking to hundreds of workers, line supervisors, CEOs, students, teachers, school and hospital administrators, doctors, and others, we will cheerfully take an oath that Drucker is right in describing the need for and role of the knowledgeable person in both worlds. Organization without knowledge leads to mindless bureaucracy, and nothing gets done; knowledge without organization leads to anarchy, and nothing gets done.

We think that Drucker includes the sense of "know-how" in his use of the world "knowledge." Dr. Myron Tribus, who describes himself as a "recovering academic," warns, "Knowledge without know-how is sterile. We use the word 'academic' in a pejorative sense to identify this limitation." Know-how is the skill required to put knowledge to work, to apply what you know to some useful purpose. To be of any value, you need both knowledge and know-how along with organization.

We suggest, however, that there is another ingredient necessary to future success, and that is by what method knowledge and organization are integrated, what management philosophy is used to bring knowledge and organization together and keep them on track and functioning. We think the quality philosophy of Dr. Deming will work best, even though—to repeat—we know it will not be easy. We've lost count of the number of senior executives who have told us that adopting the Deming philosophy was both the best and the hardest thing they had ever done. Deming is not easy to understand, principally, we

believe, because of the number of changes his management system requires—changes in what you believe, in
what you do, even in how you think about and define the
economy.

During the twentieth century, the economy could
fairly well be defined by the elements of capitalism—
money, machines, management, and manpower. Depending on how available those four elements were and how
they were blended together, economists and Wall Street
analysts could predict, or at least try to predict, how well
any company was likely to do. If a company went into
business without enough money backing it up, or if the
machinery was outdated, or if the manpower was untrained, or if the senior manager had sunk three previous
enterprises, it was reasonable to predict that the company
probably would fail. Since nothing is ever quite that obvious, the predictions of future success and failure—the
business of Wall Street—tended to be less than definitive,
but they worked well enough to keep economists, analysts, and brokers employed.

The elements of a capitalist economy are still with us
and continue to be important, even though we have to re-
name them and ruin the alliteration. With the flood of
women into the work force, *manpower* is no longer descriptive, and calling the latest-model computer or laser or
high-tech whatsis a *machine* seems pathetically under-
stated. *Money* no longer describes how companies are fi-
nanced, and most of all, *management* cannot mean in the
future what it meant in the past. Managing for quantity—
what we have done in the twentieth century—and managing for quality—what we must do in the twenty-first—are
so completely unlike that they deserve different terms to

describe them. However, even if the four classic elements of capitalism need new names, the ideas behind them are sound. You still need all four.

The difference is that they are no longer all you need.

The four elements are inadequate on their own as a basis for prediction because they leave out the two elements that matter most in the new global economy—the skills, intelligence, and motivation of the people and how they work together. They leave out knowledge and know-how. Knowledge is not a matter of manpower training or management skill. It has any number of definitions, including Deming's, which is, "Knowledge is prediction." Knowledge in the immediate future will also be the capacity to work independently or in a team, to lead or follow, to move from one task to another and to be able to do what needs to be done. That sort of employee would not fit in a traditional organization, which helps to explain why a traditional organization will not fit in the future.

Kenichi Ohmae, a Japanese consultant, author, and politician, and Robert Reich, Harvard lecturer turned secretary of labor, have been saying for several years that the single distinguishing factor of national economies that are prospering is the intelligence, skill, and motivation of the work force in each of those successful economies. Reich and Ohmae seem willing to predict future successes and failure based on knowledgeable workers, assuming that the classic elements are present. A company with no financial backing, thoroughly outdated equipment, or an incompetent senior executive is still likely to do poorly no matter what, but between two otherwise equal companies, the one with the more knowledgeable people is more likely to succeed.

As Drucker points out, knowledge without an organization in which to use that knowledge doesn't do much. He describes the new organization that will be needed to best use knowledge and says that it must feature, among other things, "continuing improvement." He says a few Japanese companies have successfully adopted continuing improvement, and he thinks the reason is "perhaps because of their Zen tradition." Zen Buddhism requires continual self-improvement through meditation to reach nirvana, but continual improvement in corporate Japan *(kaizan)* has little to do with Zen and everything to do with Deming, an American statistician and theorist (and Episcopalian, in case you care). Starting in the summer of 1950, he taught the Japanese how to do what they are doing.* The highest industrial award for excellence in Japan is the Deming Prize, established in 1951.

Obviously, the next step is to tell you what Deming did in Japan, but to do that leads to the first stumbling block to understanding. Quality—reengineering, idealized redesign, whatever you want to call it—is a relatively new field, and everyone who writes about it defines words to suit his or her needs. What we call a "system," for instance, Hammer and Champy call a "process." It doesn't matter as long as you know what the words being used mean to the people using them, so we have to define our terms.

In this book, a *process* is any action that can be repeated—hanging a door on a car on an assembly line, writing an insurance policy, taking a patient's temperature. Each is a process. If you organize two or more processes to

♦ ♦ ♦ ♦ ♦ ♦ ♦ ♦ ♦ ♦

* Deming was not alone in Japan. He was preceded by Homer Sarasohn and Charles Protzman and followed by Dr. Joseph Juran, all of whom made valuable contributions to Japanese manufacturing. The notion of continual improvement, however, belongs to Deming.

accomplish an aim, you have a *system*. The auto assembly plant, the insurance agency, and the hospital are systems. Each is an organization of many processes designed to do a specific thing. To use Deming's own definition, "A system is a network of interdependent components that work together to accomplish the aim of the system. . . . Without an aim," Deming says, "there is no system."

The aim of the system also needs to be defined; it is not what people usually call a goal. In his last book, *The New Economics for Industry, Government, Education,* Deming wrote that any system must produce something of value, must have results. Those results, the cost of achieving them, and the intended customers, he argues, will mold the aim of the system. That isn't all. "It is important," he said, "that an aim never be defined in terms of activity or methods. It must always relate directly to how life is better for everyone. . . . The aim of the system must be clear to everyone in the system. The aim must include plans for the future. The aim is a value judgment." Deming said it is management's task not only to determine the aim of the system but to manage the system to achieve that aim. "A system must be managed," he wrote. "It will not manage itself."

How you manage the system—and here's where definitions get confusing—is also a "system." Therefore, the Deming quality philosophy is a system of thinking about systems. We hoped we could solve that by using a different word for "management system," but "system" is the word Deming used, and that's that. To try to clarify the confusion, when we use the word "system" in this book, it's the organization of processes; when we use the phrase "management system" (sometimes "method"), it's the way you control the organization of processes, the management of the system, if you will. We hope that helps.

Whatever the words we use, you already know much more about this than you think you know. We accept systems without really thinking about them. Anyone who has ever played a team sport or watched one being played knows processes and systems and management systems, but no one used those words to describe what was going on. Whether it's a television network game on a Sunday afternoon or a high school game on Friday night—the sport doesn't matter—each person in the game is a process (we call them players and name their positions) and when those processes are joined, there is a system (which we call a team). The job for the management system (coaches and assistants with plans and playbooks) is to guide each process so that the system as a whole will function at its top potential (the team will play to or even beyond its rated capacity). If you understand that much, there is nothing in this chapter that you can't handle.

Deming insisted that what he taught the Japanese starting in 1950 was an entirely new management system, based at least in part on statistical analysis. The idea was that you could not consider each process complete in itself, you had to look at the system as a whole, and the system must include not only your processes but also your suppliers and customers. Your customers' likes and dislikes, wishes and desires, had to be monitored and fed back into the system so that the system would continually improve, always delighting your customers with results that exceeded their expectations.

The Deming management system includes five new ideas. First, quality does not have to cost more, as it inevitably does in a quantity system. (At a minimum, all those inspectors have to be paid.) Quality could and should cost less. Second, customers are part of the system, and, third, so are suppliers. Fourth, the ideas of customers and suppliers could be used not only to improve the product but to improve the system of making it as well. Finally, by using statistical process control to study and understand the system, you develop a way to think about how to improve the system. (Warning: Don't get hung up on statistics. Deming said that the most important numbers are "unknown and unknowable." More in chapter 3.) Put those five new ideas together, and they spell Deming's idea of continual improvement.

Continual improvement has been around for thousands of years as a concept, especially for personal behavior.* Deming's teaching in Japan is the first time we can find it used as the underlying theory of management, and he said that it was being taught no place else. Certainly, it was not being taught in the United States, where manufacturers in 1950 were still doing well with quantity manufacturing, gearing up for the Korean War. Ironically, it was Deming's work on American production standards during World War II that brought him to the attention of the Japanese when they saw those standards after the war. When Deming went to Japan, the war production standards he helped to write were not what he would teach. What the Deming management system taught the

◆　◆　◆　◆　◆　◆　◆　◆　◆

* About 1922, a French psychotherapist named Émile Coué became increasingly popular and influential in Europe and the United States by teaching that people could heal their own diseases by repeating his continual improvement slogan, "Every day, in every way, I'm getting better and better." He died in 1926.

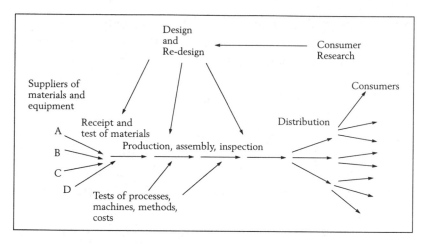

Figure 1. Production viewed as a system. Reprinted with the permission of W. Edwards Deming.

Japanese was to diagram the system with a flow chart (figure 1), so that all the people involved could see where and how they fit into the system. The chart also expanded the system by forcing the Japanese to go outside their factories to include suppliers and customers. To illustrate how far ahead of his time Deming was, Hammer and Champy complain of American firms forty-three years later, "People involved in a process [system] look *inward* toward their department and *upward* toward their boss, but no one looks *outward* toward their customer." Those using the Deming management system not only look outward toward the customer; they bring the customer into the system.

That expansion of systems to include suppliers and customers has led to new ways of thinking about organizations. To learn anything useful about General Motors, for example, you can't simply study the company, you must study it as part of the global economy, because the customers in that economy are part of the company's expanding system. (We briefly toyed with the title *The Age of Expanding Systems*, but decided that might better serve a book about the creation of the universe.)

What is critical to the success of any system, no matter what it includes, is how you manage that system. Even people who can see that a system exists in a factory (school, office, hospital, agency) will sometimes not accept what now should be self-evident: Traditional management does not and cannot get the best from any system.

The traditional way would be for every process in the system to compete to get each to do its best individually. The new way requires that each process be managed so that the system *as a whole* does its best. There is a temptation to argue that if each part is at peak efficiency, then the whole must be at peak efficiency, but that's not true. Try to imagine the cacophonous mess that would result if each member of the London Philharmonic tried to show off his or her individual musical ability rather than to play together to demonstrate the orchestra's ability. Exactly the same principle applies to any system. The goal has to be harmonious mutual benefit, and as you remember from the last chapter, that requires cooperation, not competition. It is possible to imagine a corporation in which each division is competing to do its absolute best and simultaneously destroying the organization.

With the Deming management system, it is not a question of how well each process works, the question is how well they all work *together.*

Again, what is required is a change of thinking.

Dr. Russell L. Ackoff, former dean of the Wharton School of Business, says that, since the Renaissance, mankind has used a method of thinking adapted from children. Ackoff says that when children are given a new game or toy that they need to understand, they naturally start a three-step process. "The first thing they do is take it apart," he says. "The second thing they do is try to understand the behavior of each part taken separately, and then [third] they try to aggregate the understanding of the parts into an understanding of the whole. That's analysis." Analysis has been the dominant method of Western thinking for more than four hundred years, and managers have used analysis to organize businesses and agencies. "We take corporations and schools apart into departments or disciplines," Ackoff says, "and try to run each one, and then to aggregate them into a whole. . . . That's the way we manage."

In quantity production, analysis was enough. It is not enough in quality production, which must be organized as a system, and, as Ackoff points out, "You cannot explain the behavior of a system by analysis." To explain a system, you use synthesis.* Instead of taking things apart and looking at each part separately, you put them all together and look at them as a single part of the expanded system to which they belong; that is, you expand your thinking and consider those elements that are outside what you control but that influence what you do. For instance, Ackoff likes to point out that auto mechanics can take as many English and American cars apart for as long as they like, and they will never discover why the English steering wheel is on

◆　◆　◆　◆　◆　◆　◆　◆　◆　◆

* In engineering, "synthesis" has a different meaning. If you are an engineer, where we write "synthesis," you should read "systems analysis." If you're not an engineer, ignore this footnote.

the right and the American on the left. The reason for the placement of the steering wheels was not in how the cars were assembled; the reason is in the two different societies, the expanded systems in which those cars are used.

One explanation is that in England in medieval times knights carried their lances on their right, so to joust or fight, the knights had to pass right side to right side, meaning they would have to ride to the left, as the English now drive, so that their fighting sides would be in the middle. There were no medieval knights with lances in what would become the United States. The weapons of choice here—tomahawks, six-shooters, etc.—were hand-held weapons, so to keep the "fighting hand" free and out of the enemy's reach, Americans passed left side to left side, meaning that we rode to the right, as we now drive.

It is a lovely, easily understood explanation, but prompts one troublesome question: How come the French, who had medieval knights in abundance, drive on the right?

Whatever the explanation for English and American driving preferences, the fact remains that analysis will tell you *how* cars are assembled, but synthesis will tell you *why* they are assembled that way. Analysis deals with how each part works; synthesis deals with why the parts work together, not from a mechanical point of view but from a design and function viewpoint. Synthesis is the key to a quality system. "The basic managerial idea introduced by systems thinking," Ackoff says, "is that to manage a system effectively, you might focus on the interactions of the parts rather than their behavior taken separately."

The example that both Ackoff and Deming like concerns cars again, perhaps because nearly everyone in the world has at least a vague idea of what a car is and knows more or less how a car works. In the industrial world, we have learned that some cars are better than others, and the reason some are better is the interaction of the parts. If you had automotive experts pick the world's best engine, best transmission, best axle, best everything from the cars of the world, and you assembled all those best parts, the car wouldn't work. The parts were not designed to fit together, so there is no worthwhile interaction of the parts, and the world's best car parts will not make the world's best car. If it ran at all, it would be pure luck.

Once you understand that the object must be to manage the system as a whole to achieve the best interaction of the parts, it is easier to see why so much of what American managers have tried in recent years to improve quality and productivity could not possibly work in the long run.

When American executives began to visit Japanese factories in the 1970s to find The Answer to Japan's exceptional quality in manufacturing, they first focused on quality circles, groups of Japanese factory workers who would meet to discuss problems and potential solutions and to offer suggestions for improvement in their company. When the Americans came home, quality circles began to spring up in factories, but those circles, announced with such enthusiasm, were doomed from the beginning—and not because of the workers. American workers are at least as good as their Japanese counterparts at identifying and solving problems and at making suggestions. But in Japan, quality circles were part of a management system of continual improvement that also involved management listening to the suggestions and acting on them. In the United States, quality circles were on their own; management might listen or might not, but the tradition was that managers manage and workers work. There was nothing in that tradition about managers listening to workers. The system did not allow it; therefore, there was no way quality circles could succeed.

The Americans who went to Japan had used analysis to study the system and found one part. They did not use synthesis, so they missed the whole, and in continual improvement, the whole is greater than the sum of its parts.

The other bits and pieces of highly touted techniques that came across the Pacific or were developed in the United States to improve quality and lower costs were doomed for the same reason. Just-in-time delivery, statistical process control, working with suppliers, paying attention to customers, and a dozen or more other suggestions are all worthwhile improvements, but throwing isolated improvements into a system that isn't being managed to produce quality isn't going to magically make that system produce quality. Quality comes from a management system designed to get more from the processes through cooperation than the processes can produce on their own or through competition. If every supplier a factory has delivers the goods exactly on time, every time, the factory may save money immediately by not having excess inventory, but that alone cannot improve quality in the long term. There is only a small chance that the initial savings can be sustained. Some other part of the system, overloaded by perfect deliveries it is not organized to accept or use, may well break down. To improve the system, you must have communication, coordination, and cooperation among the processes.

To produce more quality at less cost, you must reorganize the whole system; fiddling with parts of it won't do. Try it this way: If you insist on looking for individual trees, you are never going to see the forest.

To help overcome that problem, Deming made the first of his 14 Points (which we'll explain in chapter 4) "create constancy of purpose." It requires that the most senior executives of a company (or school, hospital, government agency) answer the questions "What are we doing, and why are we doing it?" * Those questions cannot be adequately answered until the system *as a whole* is studied, not by analysis, which can't answer "why" questions, but by synthesis, which can. You have to go outside and look back in. What are we doing? Why are we doing it? Instead of the standard management technique of dashing off and "doing something," the first action to take in creating a quality organization is to sit still and think. That is often difficult because another of our time-honored beliefs is "actions speak louder than words." Actions will be essential later, but without thoughtful, well-reasoned words at the beginning, quality management systems have a hard time getting started.

If you think of quality as a trip, it is difficult to persuade anyone with more sense than God gave gravel to want to go along until he or she knows where you are going and why you are going there. Knowledgeable people, who don't know where they're being taken, do not *willingly* follow anyone anywhere, and if you force them

◆　◆　◆　◆　◆　◆　◆　◆　◆　◆

*Hammer and Champy say the first question for an organization considering reengineering is "Why do we do what we do at *all*?" It seems to us to be the same question.

to go, they will become resistant and resentful. On the other hand, they become enthusiastic supporters if they are persuaded that where you are going is a better place to be.

When Deming began to consult with Ford in 1981, he asked the executives what business the Ford Motor Company was in; that is, what do you do, and why do you do it? (He knew that Ford made cars. Indeed, he had to know; he had a 1975 Ford Maverick. He still had it when he died.) What he wanted to know was what Ford senior executives thought they ought to be doing now and in the future. It took them eighteen months to give him an answer, but in the process of answering, the executives had hammered out an agreement on what they were doing and why they were doing it.

Once that agreement was reached, Ford's statement was printed on pocket-size cards and given to everyone at the company. From the most senior to the least senior employee, if anyone wanted to know what Ford was doing and what it intended to do, the answers were printed on that card. Without the thoughtful ideas the words expressed in the beginning, Ford employees might not have understood or appreciated what had to be done. Change is hard enough even when you understand why it is necessary; without that understanding, change may be impossible. To make change acceptable, the system must have an aim, and all the people in the system must understand what the aim is. The Ford statement did that.

The complete statement is in appendix A, but a brief sample will give you the idea. "Our mission is to improve continually our products and services. . . . How we accomplish our mission is as important as the mission itself." It lists its basic values as people, products, and profits, and its guiding principles are quality, customers, continual improvement, employee involvement, dealer and supplier partnerships, and integrity. It is not a list of things to do. It is a philosophical guide to excellence.

Some executives of the Hoechst Celanese Corporation have printed on the backs of their business cards twenty specific quality points under three broad headings—performance, people, and process—so that the corporation's customers will understand what Hoechst Celanese believes and how it operates. This is the briefest written statement on quality we've seen. The longest is a fourteen-page booklet published by Zytec Corporation that focuses on the company's "stakeholders," defined as "our customers, stockholders, employees, suppliers and communities." The booklet is written in simple, direct English and is remarkably free of the usual business jargon. Notice that it goes outside its own system to include not only customers and suppliers but the communities in which Zytec operates as well. It is in appendix B.

Understanding expanding systems and how they work, understanding that quality systems must be the most efficient and effective cooperative blend of their processes, is all part of "appreciation for a system." That is one of four areas you need to understand to make the Deming management system work. Deming referred to the four together as Profound Knowledge, probably for the same reason we call this the Age of Continual Improvement: You have to call it something. In one way, the name is slightly misleading. "Profound" implies some deep understanding of the four points. In truth, you can benefit with only a working knowledge of them and the recognition that they exist and affect what you do and how you do it.

You now have a working knowledge of a system. The other three points are the theory of variation, the theory of knowledge, and psychology. They are next. And as the French hero says in dated war movies . . .

Courage, mon ami!

3

• • • • •

Variation, Knowledge, and Psychology

The significant problems we face cannot
be solved at the same level of thinking we
were at when we created them.
—*Albert Einstein*

The United States suffers from severe economic and social problems. Unless those problems can be solved, today's Americans—young adults and their children—will not live as well as their parents and grandparents did. People who don't want to face that unpleasant reality always counter that Americans have faced tough problems before and have beaten them every time. That is true, but this is a different kind of problem that demands a different kind of solution. What Americans are accustomed to doing, how we traditionally solve national problems, won't work this time. Two examples ought to demonstrate the differences.

In 1862, Congress passed the Homestead Act, the Land Grant College Act, and the Pacific Railroad Act. All three were designed to open the West for settlement and, by doing that, increase agricultural production, which was essential. The population of the United States was growing more quickly than its food supply. Between 1860 and 1880, the population would increase more than 50 percent, from 31 million people to 50 million.

To get people to move westward, where the available

farmland was, the federal government promised 160 acres for a nominal fee to any settler who lived on the land and worked it for five years. Eventually, 15,000 settlers lived on 25 million acres of claims in Minnesota, Wisconsin, Kansas, and Nebraska.*

Getting people to the land wasn't the end of the problem. They had to know how to work the land, how to use new, scientific methods to reap the largest harvests. In 1862, the U.S. Department of Agriculture was established, and the Land Grant College Act gave states land to establish colleges to teach "agriculture and the mechanical [industrial] arts." Eventually, seventy-two land grant colleges would be established in the United States and its territories.

As better, more abundant crops were produced, those crops had to get to market. The Pacific Railroad Act provided land and underwrote investments for the Central Pacific and Union Pacific Railroads to build a line from Omaha to San Francisco. The line was completed in 1869.

For the three programs, the government gave away 225 million acres of public land. The federal government, in the midst of the Civil War and short of cash, guaranteed bonds for the railroads to raise private money, gave almost-free land to settlers to raise crops, and free land to states to teach those settlers how to use science to grow better crops. The historian James McPherson wrote that

♦　♦　♦　♦　♦　♦　♦　♦　♦　♦

* Settling was not merely a matter of moving. Frontier hardship, disease, and Indian attack made it dangerous. There was a Sioux uprising against settlers in Minnesota in 1862, and Custer's 7th Cavalry was wiped out at the Little Big Horn in 1876. The Indian wars did not end until the massacre at Wounded Knee in 1890.

because of those developments, the United States "became the world's breadbasket for much of the twentieth century." He also noted that because of agricultural and industrial developments started during the time of the Civil War, the United States would become the world's dominant economy before the end of the nineteenth century, succeeding Great Britain.

That's the first problem and solution. Here's the second.

In 1947, Britain's economy had been crippled by World War II, and the United States gave the government in London a loan to keep it from collapse. That wasn't enough. Every nation in Europe was on the edge of ruin, and Communists were causing trouble anywhere they could. In his Harvard commencement address that year, General George C. Marshall, then secretary of state, suggested what came to be known as the Marshall Plan. In essence, every free nation in Europe had to plan for its own long-term economic recovery, and when the plans were drawn, the United States would lend those countries the money they would need to rebuild.

By the following summer, the federal government began to pour billions of dollars into Europe, including Greece and Turkey. The historian Samuel Eliot Morison later wrote, "In retrospect, the Marshall Plan was the best thing the United States could have done for Europe." There is no question that without the Marshall Plan— which cost 80 billion of today's dollars in four years—one or more of the West European nations would have fallen to the Soviets after the war.

So we have two enormous problems faced by the United States in less than a hundred years—one internal, one external—both solved brilliantly. In each case, the solution was also a simple way to explain a fairly complex problem to the people.

President Abraham Lincoln did not have to explain the complexities of repressive European societies and governments or immigration patterns; he had only to point out that the United States was getting more people and needed more food, so if settlers were willing to grow it, the government would give them land, show them how best to cultivate it, and arrange to get their crops to market. The problem and solution are simply explained.

President Harry Truman did not have to explain political systems, economic philosophies, and future problems; he had only to say that having just fought a war to keep Europe and Asia free, the American people aren't going to let the Communists take what the Nazis could not. The United States would finance the rebuilding of a free Europe. It is a commonsense explanation and solution.

Each solution required adjustments to what Americans did and believed, but nothing more than adjustments. We had to underwrite farmers and a railroad, but the farmers still had to do the work and the capitalists still had to run the railroad. There was no radical change in what we believed or in what we did. In fact, we practiced what would increasingly become the standard American problem-solving technique so beloved by the U.S. Congress: Throw money at it.

At least three things are different this time.

First, there seems to be no simple way to explain what the problem is. When public speeches are made, they are almost inevitably about the *results* of the problem—a declining economy, expensive health care, terrible public education, increasing violent crime, and a national debt the size of Jupiter. The focus is on what is happening instead of why it is happening. There is no public recognition that all those problems have the *same root cause*. As we said at the start of chapter 1, most American managers at all levels and in all fields do not know how to manage in this new global economy. Our economy, health care, education, law enforcement, and government could all be improved by the use of a quality management system.

Second, in agriculture and foreign aid, everyone recognized the ingredients of the problems and of the solutions. No rational person in the country failed to understand that to feed more people you had to have more food. On the other hand, there is little public understanding of the need for quality management, little appreciation of what quality management could do for us, and little agreement on what quality management is. Whenever any idea labeled "quality" by any consultant, company, con man, or crackpot doesn't create instant success, all of quality is declared dead. In most places, it has not even been tried yet. People do not understand quality management because neither the press nor the politicians can explain it to them. Reporters and politicians usually define complicated issues, but this time, they don't understand it either.

Third, money cannot solve the problems, even if the government had any, which it does not. More and more people are coming to recognize that throwing money at a system does not improve the system, it only makes that system more expensive. At a Texas conference on quality in education late in 1992, Governor Ann Richards said that state spending on public schools in Texas had doubled in ten years. "Money alone will not solve the problem," Richards said, "until you change the approach and the system."

Change is required—dramatic change.

Adopting the quality system of Dr. Deming requires a personal change so radical that Deming called it transformation, a change of state, water to ice. You have to change what you believe and what you do, and no one pretends that transformation is easy. The role of what Deming called Profound Knowledge is to guide people through that transformation with as few bumps and bruises as possible. Profound Knowledge could be of interest to everyone, but it is critical for managers. Managers are not only those people who have a sufficiently grand title. Managers are everywhere, and often don't know that they are managers. Anyone who runs a household is a manager. Any teacher is a manager. Anyone who heads a volunteer program is a manager. Assuming that you do not live in a cave and subsist on berries and tree bark, the odds are that you are, have been, or will be a manager.

From the last chapter, you know about systems and expanded systems and how they can define your role. Let's have a go at the other three parts of Profound Knowledge, because each is fundamental and necessary to good management. We might just as well start with the theory of variation.

◆　◆　◆　◆　◆

Variation, as Deming used the word, appears to grow out of statistics, calculus, and biology. For us, it is easier to understand in biology, where variation recognizes that living organisms are not the same. The fact that people, including siblings, are different from each other is observable.

The statement "People are different" does not by itself provoke argument. (The argument comes, and furiously, when you try to define how they are different and explain why.) The Deming statement is essentially that direct; variation exists in all things. We often first learn about variation as children when we're told that no two snowflakes are the same. The probability is that no two people are exactly alike either and that no one person is exactly the same day to day. If you have the same person doing the same thing with the same supplies and the same machines every day, the results will be slightly different. They will not necessarily be different enough to matter, but they will be different. If you do not recognize the existence of variation, you will make expensive, not to mention stupid, mistakes.

In chapter 2, we said that the object of the exercise was to run the processes so that the system as a whole was at its most effective. You can't do that until you know how well each process is capable of doing. To put it another way, you need to know the predictable variation inherent in what you are doing, and as good fortune would have it, variation can be measured rather easily. Deming started by realizing that if variation could be measured, you could know how to improve the system by reducing the amount of variation in each process. If you don't know how much variation exists, you can't possibly know how to reduce it. Even worse, you can't be certain whether the process is stable—that is, predictable—or whether it is totally out of control. That is part of the lesson of Deming's Red Bead Experiment, which took a full day at Deming's four-day seminar. It's a wonderful way to learn, because it is not only a clear illustration of the theories involved, it's great fun as well.

It started when Deming asked for volunteers from the seminar audience. He needed six Willing Workers, two inspectors, a chief inspector, and a record keeper. On a long table, he put two plastic containers about the size of small dish-washing pans, and a paddle with holes. One of the containers held red and white beads, marble-size, that would rest in the holes in the paddle. The paddle had fifty of those holes. (At one seminar, Deming put the paddle on an overhead projector, so the students could see its outline and the holes, and asked if anyone could explain why, for this experiment, the paddle had fifty holes. After a couple of incomprehensible, statistically motivated guesses from the audience, Deming smiled and said, "Because it has five rows of ten holes." Mathematical humor.)

Deming carefully explained to the volunteers that they are now in a factory, that Deming is the boss, and that the job of the factory is to make white beads—white beads and only white beads. There is no market for red beads. He gave them specific, ridiculously detailed instructions on exactly how each Willing Worker was to pour the beads from one container to the other, precisely how to insert the paddle into the beads, scoop in one direction and collect fifty of them, then gently shake excess beads back into the container. The instructions represented the standard operation procedures for the make-believe plant.

With the paddle containing fifty beads held carefully to prevent any loss of beads, each Willing Worker went in turn to the two inspectors, who counted the red beads, the bad ones, on the paddle. When they agreed, they told the senior inspector, who inspected the inspectors' work, certified the count, then gave it to the recorder, who wrote it under the employee's name on the overhead projector. That represented one day's work. The worker returned the beads to the bucket and handed the paddle to the next Willing Worker, who started the process again. Deming praised those who got only a few red beads, and gently (on the first pass) asked those who got a lot of red beads to try harder on the second and subsequent scoops. He reminded them that their future and the plant's success depended entirely on their hard work.

From that simple description, no one would believe how intense this make-believe becomes. One Willing Worker was fired for trying to bribe an inspector—and he meant it! It was not a joke. He would have *paid* for a good count. Another Willing Worker wrote Deming to say that even though she knew it was a game she could not win, her pride became so involved in producing white beads that it was all she could focus on. Producing white beads became a cause, a challenge. Every red bead was a personal affront.

As the workers tried harder and harder, getting more or fewer red beads in no perceptible pattern, Deming went through all the standard management techniques. He promised bonuses for fewer red beads, threatened dismissal for more, pleaded that the factory would have to close, praised the good workers, threatened the bad ones. When a worker who did well on one scoop did poorly on the next, Deming stopped the assembly line and demanded to know what went wrong. After the third round, he fired the three worst workers—the ones who had scooped up the most red beads on average—and kept the factory open with the three workers who had produced the highest percentage of white beads. It didn't matter; red beads continued to show up in unacceptable and unpredictable quantities. Nothing worked, not even the cheers and boos of the audience, who were as caught up in the game as were the Willing Workers. In the end, the factory closed because the Willing Workers were not willing to produce only white beads.

They could not. It's impossible.

The containers hold four times as many white beads as red ones—3,200 to 800—but the mix guarantees that it is statistically impossible to get no red bead on any single scoop, and it is highly improbable that you'll get more than 18. The Willing Workers cannot produce only white beads because of the way the "factory" is organized. No system can produce greater quality than it is organized to produce. Blaming workers for the organization of the plant is futile. There is nothing they can do about it. If management wants higher quality, management must reorganize the system. When you hear some executive blaming a lack of quality on his workers, bet everything you own that the workers aren't the problem. Deming said that where there is a quality problem, there is an 85-to-94 percent probability that management caused it—is not simply responsible for it, but *actively caused it*. That is the first lesson of the red beads.

Since the number of red beads is predictable within statistical limits—one to eighteen per scoop—the process is said to be stable. You can predict what is going to happen every time, and you will almost always be right. As an indication of how often you will be right in your prediction, Deming did the Red Bead Experiment thousands of times. The number of red beads in one scoop has exceeded eighteen exactly once. There has never been no red bead. The scoop of fifty will not inevitably produce one to eighteen red beads, but that's the way to bet.*

Asked to explain why that one time there were more than eighteen red beads, Deming shrugged and said, "I don't know." It was obvious that he was not going to waste any time trying to find out. Whatever it was, it was a special cause of variation and trying to find out why it happened, when it may never happen again, is wasteful and, in all probability, fruitless. If a special cause can't be spotted immediately, it may never be found. Understanding that concept is part of the theory of variation. Special causes are often, even usually, unavoidable. In most cases, it isn't going to happen again anyway because it isn't built into the system. Common causes are built into the system and are going to exist forever unless they are eliminated; that is, some part of the process or system has to be improved. The most obvious common cause in the Red Bead Experiment is that there are red beads in the mix, and if you want to reduce the predictable proportion of red beads that each scoop will produce, one way is to reduce the number of, or eliminate, red beads in the container.

Notice that the workers are not permitted to alter the mix of red and white beads. Beads are supplies, and management controls what is bought from whom; workers have nothing to do with negotiating or writing contracts with the suppliers. It is another example of Deming's oft-repeated point that most problems are caused by the system, management is responsible for the system, and, therefore, management is responsible for most problems.

◆　◆　◆　◆　◆　◆　◆　◆　◆　◆

* When reminded of Ecclesiastes 9:11, "The race is not [always] to the swift, nor the battle to the strong," some sage is alleged to have replied, "Yeah, but that's the way to bet."

A U.S. Navy document on quality says, "Common causes of variation exist because of the system or the way the system is managed. These causes are beyond the reach of the workers and only those who manage or control the system are responsible for them." Managers often resent being told that, but we know of no one who has ever been able to refute it.

One thing more. Over the years, Deming used three different paddles to scoop beads, and he kept a careful tally of the number of beads in every scoop. The average number of red beads is different for each paddle. Unless you can believe that plastic magically attracts more red beads than apple wood, the obvious reason is variation.

Most American managers cannot tell you with any certainty what each process in their system will produce. They don't know, they don't know how to find out, and if asked what causes the variation, they will usually blame it on the workers who won't follow standard procedures, don't try hard enough, or are stupid, saboteurs, malcontents, or all of the above. The idea that variation exists and can be accurately measured seems foreign to them.

One other point about variation. Let us assume that you control a system made up of twelve processes. You want them to be managed in a way that will produce what is best, so what you want is cooperation among the twelve. You will have to work at it. You will have to work very hard. Because the world is perverse and life is not fair, what you must work very hard to get, variation seems to negatively create—a kind of cooperation for harm driven by Murphy's Law. It works this way: A tiny, all-but-imperceptible imperfection in step one may make an even smaller imperfection in step two much worse than it otherwise would have been, which turns an all but infinitesimal variant in step three into a huge defect, and so on through the twelve steps until by the end, not one damned thing works, but each step has been only a hairsbreadth off the mark. Welcome to the world of the Taguchi Loss Function, which is all about how little faults grow geometrically to become an enormous headache, also known as the interaction of forces, part of the theory of variation. It is not the same as, but it is reminiscent of, the adage that starts "For want of a nail . . ." and ends with a failed battle. The little stuff just beats you to death.

There is more to variation than that, but that's enough to give you an idea of how variation works with things. Variation is even more complex with people. No two people are alike, and saying that does not mean that you are rating the two or comparing them; you are observing a physical fact, nothing more. Another fact is that no one person is exactly the same day to day or even hour to hour. To believe that all people will react the same way to any event or that one person will react exactly the same way on two different days is to admit that you know nothing about people. It was the theory of variation and special and common causes that led Deming to realize that merit pay and other systems of rewards, along with annual personal appraisals and rankings, were common causes that prevented people from cooperating within the system. Deming wrote, "The most important application of the principles of statistical control of quality, by which I mean knowledge about common causes and special causes, is in the management of people." He said that applying his theory to the shop floor, by which he meant the processes that produce things and can be measured, would yield a 3 percent overall benefit. Applying them to the people and the processes that affect people would give a 97 percent benefit. Some people find that surprising, but the idea that people are more important than things is hardly news.

Here is the immediate and obvious problem: The variations in people and their daily actions, reactions, and interactions defy any attempt to measure them with pinpoint or, for that matter, even ballpark accuracy. What to do? As they are wont to say in late-night television ads, relief is in sight—reach for the theory of knowledge.

◆ ◆ ◆ ◆ ◆

Understanding requires theory, some basic assumption, hunch, or idea against which you can test experiences and examples. Deming was fond of telling seminar students, "Experience teaches nothing without theory." What he was talking about is not the theory of relativity or the theory of games or any of the other grand ideas of the age that many of us don't understand and never will. Nonetheless, most of us have perfectly valid theories. They are part of our lives; they are assumptions we make and principles we apply that help us explain what goes on. We need them to learn, and we all have them, but we have not routinely thought about them as theories. We have to begin to do that, to realize that we operate with theory, and, by definition, no theory can ever be proved, so we have to be prepared to modify our theories when they become outdated.

In chapter 1, we talked about all the beliefs we have that hold us back. Those are theories we believe that now are proved inaccurate. For instance, our theory has been that competition brings out the best in people. It is now demonstrated that cooperation brings out the best in people; therefore, we have to modify our theory. We normally call that "changing my mind" or "learning something new," and it seems a bit pretentious to call it "modifying a theory." As with other things, what you call it is not as important as the fact that you know it.

Most parts of the theory of knowledge you already know, even though you may not know that you know them. For instance, you may not immediately accept Deming's statement that any plan requires prediction, even if the plan is only to go home for lunch. What prediction? Without thinking about it, you have made an incredible number of them. You predict that you will be able to leave your office and building. Your car will be where you left it and will start and run. The streets between your office and home will be open and functional. You will not run into another car; another car will not run into you. Traffic police will not stop you, a parade will not delay you, and rioting potato farmers will not turn your car over and set it on fire. You will arrive home. You will be able to get into your home; that is, your spouse has not had the locks changed in your absence. There will be something to eat. You will be able to eat it. And that's only a few of the predictions you've made. Theory is prediction, because it not only describes what is happening now, but what we expect will happen if a similar set of circumstances occurs in the future.

In short, prediction is life, but you don't define prediction or life that way. Which raises another point. The necessity for definitions is also part of the theory of knowledge. For any communication to occur, you and another person must agree on definitions, and definitions depend on individual assumptions and beliefs (theories). Even when you agree on definitions, there is no guarantee of understanding if the two of you have different theories about what those definitions actually mean. Consultant William W. Scherkenbach quotes a Ford vice president as saying, "I know what I told our buyers; I do not know what they heard." If the buyers have different theories, then they did not hear what the vice president meant. Deborah Tannen wrote the book *You Just Don't Understand: Women and Men in Conversation* about the fact that men and women do not communicate in the same way and do not necessarily mean the same things even when they use exactly the same words. Greg Howard ends one of his "Sally Forth" comic strips about a young married couple with the statement that between men and women "talking and communicating are two different animals." If the problem existed only between men and women, it might be easier to solve.* It exists between and among us all.

The theory of knowledge becomes difficult for most people to understand when they have to accept the idea that if you observe it or measure it the observation or measurement does not have a true value. (Yes, we know that's the dumbest-sounding sentence you ever read, but hang in there; it makes more sense than it seems to.) If someone else looks at the same thing you look at, he or she will see something other than what you see, even though you may agree in words on what you both are looking at. If you buy a Ferrari, and everyone agrees that a Ferrari is exactly what is parked at the curb, each of you will "see" something else. You may see it as an indication of your financial success and a symbol of your admiration

◆　◆　◆　◆　◆　◆　◆　◆　◆　◆

* Or on second thought, it might not.

of automotive excellence. Your spouse may see it as an incomprehensible waste of money, your children may see your enfeebled attempt to recapture a lost youth, your boss may see that you are overpaid or embezzling, and your mechanic will definitely see the braces he needs for his kid's teeth. Every one of you will agree that you see a Ferrari; no two of you will observe the same thing. Despite that, you did buy a Ferrari. The different theories about why you bought it don't matter unless all of you are working together on some improvement project involving either you or the car. If you are working together, then the lack of a definition of "Ferrari" could well destroy any hope of success. If you are not working together, then the different definitions, if you learned about them, would be only a mild slap to your ego. Either way, however, your bank account took a body blow.*

With measurement you have a slightly different situation. The figure you get will change if you change the way you measure. Any count you get will change if you change the way you count. Reporters are probably more able to accept that than most people because for years we have listened to different groups tell us how many people were in the same crowd. No two of them ever agreed. Which does not alter the fact that there were some people, and they were all assembled at one place for some purpose. That is information, not knowledge. To use one of Deming's examples, a dictionary is loaded with information, but it contains no knowledge.

As a practical matter, you can use this observation and

◆　◆　◆　◆　◆　◆　◆　◆　◆　◆

* A 1992 Ferrari F-40 sold new for $450,000 to $475,000. It doesn't have any bathrooms.

measurement, but you have to accept that somewhere along the line you may have to change. Part of knowledge is the ability and the willingness to question what you are certain that you "know." As Deming said, "We 'know' so much that isn't so." As we said in chapter 1, clinging to what we "know" is what helps hold us back now. That gets us to people and why they act the way they do, which is the final part of Profound Knowledge.

* * * * *

A basic point in the theory of psychology grows out of the theories of knowledge and of variation. It says simply that people are different, that they learn at different speeds and in different ways, and no way of learning is better or worse than any other way. There is a temptation to say, "So what?"—but think about how schools are organized, how companies train new employees, how the armed services run training schools. The central idea in each case is not to make it easy for the student to learn; the central idea is to make it easy for the organization to teach. That is an enormous, and potentially damaging, difference, and it is caused by not understanding that people learn at different speeds in different ways.

An even larger potentially damaging misunderstanding is about motivation, which is also part of Deming's theory of psychology. To prevent any possible confusion, psychology in Profound Knowledge is about everyday people and how they react and interact in various situations. This is not psychiatry, which deals with mental and emotional disorder and disease. What we're talking about is often taught in college as Industrial Psychology 101, and it is designed to answer the connected questions "How do I get the best from people? How do I give the best to people?"

In the United States, the answer to both questions has almost always been money. There is growing evidence that money may be the wrong answer. Obviously, people have basic needs and those needs must be met, and until they are met, nothing else can happen. A worker who can't pay the rent or buy food or heat his home is highly unlikely to think about how to do a job better for his company. Quality of life is a great motivation, and until that quality of life is reasonable, no other motivation makes any difference. However, once your needs are met, money may not be the best motivation. N. L. "Norb" Keller, who was director of materials management for one of the divisions at the time, told a GM meeting in November 1987, "If General Motors were to double the pay of everybody at General Motors beginning the first of December, nothing would change. Performance would be exactly what it is now." Colleagues at GM admitted that he was right, although no one would have objected to double pay.

Merit pay programs are even less reliable. Charles Peck, a senior research associate with The Conference Board, a New York–based business research group, concluded in a book review, "Merit pay is dubious in theory, unverifiable experimentally, and subject to all sorts of contaminants in practice." He does not like merit pay, but he suggests alternatives or improvements that, he says, might be better. Deming believed merit pay or anything that resembled merit pay should be abolished, along with anything else that got in the way of group cooperation, such as personnel rankings or appraisals. As we mentioned in chapter 1 in talking about scapegoats, if the system is principally responsible for what kind of work is produced, why are the workers rewarded or punished? Why would they be rated?

Obviously, good and bad individual work can be done, and the manager's job is to encourage the good and eliminate the bad. To do that, the manager has to be aware that there are intrinsic and extrinsic motivations—the needs we have inside, and the forces from outside (the system and the expanded system)—and the manager has to remember variation and realize that people will react differently and will have different needs. In one important way, however, we are all pretty much alike. To a greater or lesser degree, all of us would like to be appreciated. For each person there is a blend of external and internal motivations, a balance that meets each of our needs to feel good about what we do and know that others feel good about us.

When those conditions are met, when we feel we are appreciated, we tend to do more than is strictly necessary. We do discretionary work that we can do or not, as we please, and no one else will know. For instance, a design engineer staring at a pad and thinking looks exactly the same whether the engineer is planning a hot, new product or a hot, new date. The more of the engineer's motivational needs that have been met, the more likely it is that a product is being considered, and that is high-value, discretionary work that cannot be had in any other way. The engineer gives it, or does not, and that's the end of that. "One is born with a natural inclination to learn and be innovative." Deming said, "One inherits a right to joy in his work. Psychology helps us to nurture and preserve these positive innate attributes of people."

Again, don't read this as being more complicated or grander than it is. All we are saying is that a person may feel good that he was able to accomplish something, but he may feel even better if someone whose opinion he respects praises the way he did it. It is that simple.

There are two dangers. First, the internal motivations can be overshadowed by external ones, and, second, the external reward can be out of proportion or misplaced. In either case internal motivations can be damaged, and they are the ones we are born with, the only ones on which we can rely throughout life. As bad fortune would have it, society is organized to provide more external than internal motivation, from gold stars for attendance at school to prizes for the best Halloween costume, from merit pay to grander titles. If we become accustomed to the idea of external rewards, inevitably, when there is not one, we will be devastated. The last thing anyone needs in any organization is even one person who doubts his or her own value or importance. Being aware of the theory of psychology and the theory of variation might prevent that from happening.

◆　◆　◆　◆　◆

Deming did not teach Profound Knowledge to the Japanese. He did not even name its four parts until the late 1980s, and we believe it defines his quality management system in a way that those of us who are not statisticians can understand. It helps people see how they can simultaneously and systematically manage an organization and build this new management system into it. It helps people understand the nuances of a flow chart, like the one drawn on a blackboard in a steamy classroom in Tokyo in August 1950. It helps people understand what the Deming management system is trying to do and how it is trying to do it. The theories of systems, variation, knowledge, and psychology are not yet as well known, but they are at least as important to the future as money, machines, management, and manpower were to the past.

Now that you know the four parts, it would be fun to know how to apply them. That's next, when we talk about the 14 Points.

4

· · · · ·

The 14 Points

It is possible to fly without motors,
but not without knowledge and skill.
—*Wilbur Wright*

It is at about this point that some people begin to feel a sense of frustration. They know the beliefs they'll have to change, they understand systems, and they have at least a nodding acquaintanceship with the theories of variation, knowledge, and psychology. They know that they need to change; the problem is that they do not know how, and they inevitably ask, "What do we *do*?" Dr. Deming did not provide a recipe. He wanted you to think about what you are doing. You are not likely to think if you are intent on following a list of prescribed steps and trying to match what is happening with what has been forecast to happen. (Since every organization has different problems and potentials, whatever is forecast to happen may not anyway.) However, while he gave no recipe, Deming does help you focus your thoughts with his 14 Points, which he developed in the late 1970s to better teach his quality management system. They are something like rules of the road for achieving quality. Rules of the road won't make you a good driver, but it's difficult to imagine a good driver who doesn't know them.

If you consider the 14 Points as a group, rather than as disparate bits of information, you'll find that they represent a philosophy, a logical, humane, and pleasant way to get things done. They specify ways to apply Profound Knowledge.

We said in chapter 3 that Profound Knowledge is a must for *managers*, although we define "managers" to include a good many more people than those who carry the title. The 14 Points are a must for *everyone*. Each of the points sounds reasonably straightforward, even simple in some cases, but each also represents a change in the way things are commonly done in the United States.

◆ ◆ ◆

1. Create Constancy of Purpose

This point was mentioned in chapter 2. You have to answer two questions: What are we doing? Why are we doing it? You must have a long-term aim, something that every member of the organization knows and can understand. It must have meaning. It must be concerned with the future. It must be aimed at keeping you in business, making a profit, and making life better for your customers.

In chapter 1, we mentioned "delight factors," things you give the customer that he or she did not expect. That grows out of constancy of purpose. You give the customer something unexpected, because you know what you can develop and the customer does not. One of Deming's answers when he was asked about this point was, "Who asked for the electric light? The customer does not know what you can do for him." Constancy of purpose requires that you stay ahead of your market. It does not require that you worry about Wall

Street. In quantity management, you look to Wall Street, then go to the market.

At this point, traditional American managers, stockbrokers, and some stockholders tend to fume and splutter, but constancy of purpose is long-term, and Wall Street is short-term. Wall Street survives on quarterly reports, but in quality management systems quarterly reports are all but meaningless. People who are involved in financial manipulation to make the *figures* look good cannot simultaneously be involved in those areas that will make the *future* look good. However, in your zeal to transform, don't try to go from one extreme to the other. As a practical matter, you cannot ignore Wall Street. You must keep in mind that you cannot prosper in the future if you go bankrupt in the meantime. You must make a profit; you must intend to stay in business making a profit in the future. Deming told his audiences to think of it as "Open for business during renovations."

◆ ◆ ◆

2. Learn the New Philosophy

The old philosophy is to compete. The new philosophy is to cooperate in the organization so that everyone can win. For that to happen there must be a determination of what is needed, an organization to achieve what is needed, and the knowledge and the know-how to get it done. All of that grows from the desire to adopt a quality management system, but desire by itself is not enough. You must know how to go about it. The Deming system has to be learned, then taught to everyone in the system, including suppliers.

As an example of how Profound Knowledge and the 14 Points work together, you can see how part of the theory of psychology is important in this point. As you are teaching the new philosophy, you must remember that people learn in different ways and at different speeds. You will have immediate enthusiastic supporters, you will have doubters, and you will have opponents. Some people will be thrilled; some will be terrified. You have to know that is going to happen and plan for it. Just because you think a quality management system is a great idea does not mean that everyone thinks so. (It's disheartening, but there it is, nonetheless.)

◆ ◆ ◆

3. Cease Dependence on Mass Inspection

Inspection does not add quality. Inspections tells you if quality is there. It is or is not, and inspection cannot change it either way. Inspection may be, at least in theory, one way to ensure quality to the customer, but it is expensive and often unreliable. You have to pay the inspectors, and you have to correct the mistakes that they find. Because you understand variation, you know that the inspectors themselves will be sharper some days than others, so even if they always try to do their best, some bad bit will occasionally get through. Inspectors will be more or less rigorous for a variety of reasons, and the costs of inspection will go up and down accordingly.

The most obvious place where this point is being ignored in current debate is in secondary education, where citizens are at each other's throats over whether there should or should not be a national test before American students graduate from high school.

A test is inspection. It cannot make any student more intelligent. It can only point out which ones have mastered the material and which have not—any of the kids' teachers could have told you for free—or perhaps it can indicate which students know how to take tests well and which ones don't. Having taken the National Honest-to-God Whizbang Test to Make Education Better, no student in the United States will be smarter or dumber than he or she was before taking the test. The cost of education will have gone up because someone has to prepare, administer, and grade the tests. Remember, inspectors must be paid.

It is also absolutely predictable that if enough students fail the test, the result will not be a more rigorous education but a less rigorous test. (That is an even better bet than predicting the number of red beads in each scoop of fifty.) Public education will have become both more expensive and worse because Deming's third point was ignored—again.

◆ ◆ ◆

4. Don't Buy on Price Tag Alone

This one used to send purchasing agents into pure fits, but more and more companies are finding out that it actually works. The cost of anything is not the initial price, but the initial price *plus* how much you have to pay over the life of the product for maintenance and repair. Buying the cheapest supplies may often raise your actual costs.

Deming told of a shoe company that saw a sudden, dramatic drop in its productivity. What had happened, he discovered, was that an eager young purchasing agent had found thread for a penny-a-bobbin cheaper. It takes an enormous amount of thread to make certain models of shoes, particularly men's shoes, and while a penny isn't much money, multiplied by millions of bobbins, a penny becomes big bucks. The new thread cost a penny less because it wasn't as well made. It would break. Sewing-machine operators had to stop and rethread their industrial sewing machines. Productivity and profits dropped because one person looked at the price tag on the bobbin of thread and did not consider what the company would actually pay for it in lost productivity. What you must learn to do is ignore how much it costs and consider how much it is worth.

The way to get the least expensive, best supplies is to work with one supplier for each item in a long-term relationship. Assured of your business, that supplier can concentrate on improvement of his own system to produce what you need at a reasonable cost. By working together, you may find more effective methods to reduce costs for both while both of you improve your products. Several companies now include suppliers in initial design conferences so they can suggest ways to hold down costs with better-designed supplies. Just as you know more about what you can give to your customers than your customer knows, it is also true that your suppliers know more about what they can give to you than you know. You are their customer, and your needs and ideas must be fed back into their systems if they are to improve their quality and help you improve yours. They cannot do that if you won't let them.

◆ ◆ ◆

5. Improve Constantly Every Process

This point is often misunderstood. Critics claim that a quality management system won't work because continual improvement gives you only incremental improvements when what you need is an enormous leap forward. That criticism is misplaced. You do get those leap-forward improvements with the Deming management system, but you *also* get the smaller improvements between the leaps. If you achieve only one massive improvement and do not follow up that success, you will eventually wind up with another problem. This year's state of the art is next year's passé. If you get a massive improvement *and* never stop trying to make it better, you do not wind up with another problem because the process and the system never settle back into a rut, even a much advanced rut. That's the reason we say that the Deming management system may be the first solution that does not have a future problem built in.

Continual improvement (point 5) is the way to cease mass inspection (point 3), but to do either you will need to look at the overall price, not just the price tag (point 4) of supplies, none of which you would even consider doing if you had not learned the win-win philosophy (point 2) and determined what your purpose is (point 1). Each of the 14 points ties in with one or more of the others. These are not disconnected steps. The 14 Points represent an integrated way to change from an internally competitive system to an internally cooperative system. Guided by Profound Knowledge, you are trying to change the culture in which you operate, and that is never easy to do.

◆　◆　◆

6. Institute Training for Skills

Robert Reich, before he was secretary of labor, said, "Your most precious possession is not your financial assets. Your most precious possession is the people you have working there, and what they carry around in their heads, and their ability to work together." Job-skill training is one part of that, both for management and for labor. The Deming method says that part of that training is about how to do the job and another part is about why the job is being done. Unless everyone knows why they are doing a job, they cannot do it well. They have to know the aim of the system and where their tasks fit in.

The typical way to train new employees is to have them watch old employees. Think back to chapter 3 and the interaction of forces where one little mistake interacts with other little mistakes to build a massive problem. When new employees are trained by old employees, not only will the new employees learn the old employees' mistakes, they will create their own new variations. In the end, they will have been "trained," after the standard American fashion, but they will have no idea what they are doing and no idea why they are doing it.

Training is more extensive in a quality management system because it must include both training for the necessary specific skills and training in teamwork and communication. It does no good if some worker has the best idea of the decade but does not have the verbal or written skills to take the idea to someone who can do something about it. The worker also needs the confidence to communicate that idea, which comes from working within a system where management has made it clear that ideas are welcomed and will be respected.

Once each worker learns all the skills necessary to do the job, there is no need to continue skills training. Additional training will be necessary if there are changes in the process or in the people doing the work.

◆ ◆ ◆

7. Institute Leadership

Training for management must include training for leadership, an altogether different skill from what has normally been required, which is supervision. Deming believed the American worker, when properly led, not driven, is the best in the world, so leadership must replace supervision. "What leadership must do," Deming said, "is to help people." Reich said some years ago, "A leader is someone who steps back from the entire system and tries to build a more collaborative, more innovative system that will last over the long term. . . . I suspect that if we do get leadership, and the kind of leadership that Dr. Deming is talking about, we will see things like a more collaborative work force, less of a distinction between management and labor."

The idea is to help all people do a better job, recognizing their different "abilities, capabilities, and aspirations." Having people in the organization highly trained (point 6) isn't going to pay off as it should unless they are also well led. They will not be well led unless they are ethically led. We'll discuss this in a later chapter, but we ought to mention here that in all our travels around the world, we have never found a quality company that was not also an ethical company. One of Deming's favorite comments was that the senior executive can no more delegate the responsibility for quality than he or she can delegate the responsibility for ethics. Both come from the top and are necessary elements of leadership.

There is one special area of concern when you are changing from supervision to leadership.

Supervisors were hired because they had the capability to give orders and have those orders obeyed, sometimes with a pat on the back and a joke, sometimes with curt orders and a threat. Those men and women, however they got their orders obeyed, kept America's mass-production factories turning out goods, and without those supervisors, America's quantity production system could not have functioned as well as it did. What happens to those supervisors now?

When an organization incorporates a quality management system, the odds are that the greatest resistance will come from middle managers and supervisors. Senior management has already accepted the idea and agreed to a quality system or it wouldn't be starting. Most workers accept the idea quickly, perhaps because they recognize that they have little to lose and a lot to gain. Middle managers and supervisors may have a lot to lose, and initially they'll feel threatened. If they have sense enough to hold their jobs, they also have sense enough to figure out that those jobs will no longer be needed. They will have to be trained for leadership, to do new and necessary jobs. Without that training, you will leave supervisors and middle managers resentful and afraid, which gets us to the next point.

◆ ◆ ◆

8. Drive out Fear

"Point 8," Deming says, "is to drive out fear, build trust.
. . . It's purely a matter of management." Peter Scholtes,
the consultant, says, "To lead a company focused on improvement requires a whole different set of values and attitudes and relationships than leading an organization
focused on control." If you're about to say that Scholtes'
comment ought to be back up under point 7, this is the
time to tell you that if you read over the 14 Points and
consider the implications of each, you'll find that driving
out fear is part of at least nine of them, not counting this
one. "The waste due to fear is enormous," William
Scherkenbach wrote. "It is one of those invisible figures,
however, and thus doesn't get management's immediate
attention."

Fear is a method of control and directly opposite what
the Deming method teaches. He insisted that everyone in
an organization must cooperate in a sense of mutual trust
and respect. That is not possible if you are afraid that if
you help someone solve a problem the person you help
may get a higher annual personal rating than you, thus a
higher merit pay increase. It isn't that you are selfish and
don't want to help; you are afraid to. You are in a win-lose
situation, and you are afraid to lose, which makes sense
under the circumstances.

Another case: You know that something is about to go
wrong, but you also know that the CEO hates bad news
and the people who bring it to him. If you tell him, the
problem might be solved before any harm is done. Or, if
you tell him, he may ignore the information and punish

you for spoiling his day. When whatever you said might go wrong does go wrong, he may punish you again for not making him understand how critical it was. You are afraid, which makes sense under the circumstances.

You are a well-trained, highly motivated, rock-hard, leather-lunged, veteran line supervisor who gives crisp, clear orders and insists on and gets instant obedience. You are told that the company is about to start a new quality management system, one result of which will be that no one will be needed to give orders on the line. You are afraid, which happens to be reasonable under the circumstances.

Those cases are clear. The source of fear in each case is immediate and obvious. The idea is not to be without fear, but to know how to manage it. "I personally don't think fear will ever be driven from the workplace," Scherkenbach wrote. Nor does it need to be. There will always be a certain amount of fear in work, but the problems come when actions are *based* on fear. Decisions based on fear inevitably are intended not to accomplish something positive, but to avoid anything negative.

Another part of fear in this context is anxiety. You don't know exactly why you are afraid, but you are; you know something bad is about to happen, even if you don't quite know what. Anxiety is often a deliberate part of some corporate cultures, especially in those organizations where information is not shared, where people have no way to ask questions and get answers, where firings and layoffs occur for no apparent reason, and where senior management is as remote and as arbitrary as the gods.

A company driven by fear or anxiety will never have quality management because, as Dr. Gipsie Ranney, a professor and consultant says, "You can't address the technical problems of quality without addressing the social systems of the organization."

A quality management system cannot exist where fear is a method of control or where, as Scherkenbach pointed out, "an atmosphere of mutual respect" does not exist. For a quality management system to succeed, people at all levels must feel secure enough in themselves and their jobs to cooperate fully and to point out problems and suggest solutions.

• • •

9. Break Down Barriers Between Staff Areas

"Build a system within your organization," Deming said, "for win-win. This means cooperation. It means abolishment of competition." Think back to chapter 2. Everything is a system and must be organized for the best *overall* performance, which requires that every part of the system has to cooperate for the benefit of the system. Most American organizations are divided into divisions and departments, each of which competes against the others for its own benefit. Each department guards its own budget and tries to get more even if the money might better be spent somewhere else. The agent who almost put the shoe company out of business (in point 4) bought cheaper thread to make the purchasing department look good by saving money on supplies. Had he been cooperating with manufacturing for the benefit of the company, one test on one bobbin of thread would have prevented the problem and saved the company enormous amounts of money. Equally important, it would have saved the workers weeks of growing anger and frustration as they were prevented by poor supplies from doing their best work.

Another problem of divisional or departmental competition is the internal politics wars it inevitably causes. Anyone who knows corporate politics knows that if you cannot make yourself look better, the next best thing is to make an internal rival look worse. Never mind what that does to the company; it keeps him from getting ahead of you. If you are about to say that is neither fair nor ethical, you are right. Irrelevant, but right; it is going to happen. Truth is the first casualty of war,* and while ethics may not be the *first* casualty of competition, ethics will be a casualty.

If you want people to think always of the good of the company, you must make it possible for them to do so, and they cannot if you require them to compete. Think about psychology for a moment, and you will realize that it is unrealistic to expect ordinary people to act like selfless saints. That's one reason why there are so few saints; if it were easy, there would be a lot more of them.

◆ ◆ ◆

10. Eliminate Slogans, Exhortations, and Targets

When some company puts up a banner that reads, IM-PROVE PRODUCTIVITY 10 PERCENT IN '95, there is an immediate and painfully obvious question: If it were that easy—put up a sign and get results—why didn't the com-

◆ ◆ ◆ ◆ ◆ ◆ ◆ ◆ ◆ ◆

* In a speech in the U.S. Senate in 1917, Senator Hiram Johnson said, "The first casualty when war comes is truth."

pany put up the sign last year? Why wait until now? Why not make it 20 percent? How about 100 percent? Would it happen faster if the sign were bigger? If the letters were red? If it promised a reward or a punishment?

Slogans, exhortations, and targets do not answer the question Deming was so fond of asking: "By what method?" *How* are you going to increase productivity? If the supplies are shoddy, the work force untrained and fearful, the machines out of control, and the management system chaotic, productivity is not going to be increased by anything other than pure luck, and if you are that lucky, you don't need the banner to begin with.

A mild caution. This does not mean you cannot have a poster or banner that states the company aim or recognizes company successes or provides information all personnel need. Point 10 is not against banners, it is against blaming the workers for a lack of quality or suggesting that achieving quality and success are entirely in the workers' hands.

If the system has not been organized to produce quality, there is nothing the workers can do about it. Putting up a banner that somehow suggests it is all their fault will either anger or demoralize them, which all but guarantees that productivity will go down, not up. However, look on the bright side: If it goes down 10 percent, you can always point out to your boss that you had the amount right, only the direction was wrong. It *might* work, and the argument is certainly no sillier than believing that slogans produce quality.

• • •

11. Eliminate Numerical Goals and Quotas

The argument is the same as for point 10. If all you had to do was establish a numerical goal, why did you not do it last year? Why don't you increase the number and get even more?

Deming talked about an airline information and reservations agent who had been told that she had two job requirements—satisfy the calling customers and take twenty-five calls each hour. The problem is that she cannot know what her job is. Is it to satisfy the customers every time or is it to take twenty-five calls every hour? It cannot be both. In a good hour when every caller knew exactly what he or she wanted, the agent might satisfy her callers and take thirty calls. But what if she has to be rude to one customer to get that twenty-fifth call in? Will she have helped the airline, her employer, stay in business and helped herself keep her job? If the customer to whom she was rude vows never to buy a ticket on that airline again and tries to persuade others to shun it as well, was that twenty-fifth call worth it? That is one of those figures that falls into Deming's "unknown and unknowable" category. What is a lost customer worth?

In a quality management system, everyone is aware that sufficient product must be produced to satisfy customer orders, but the focus is on how well the product is made. Quality is more important than quantity. Numerical goals and quotas are a hangover from mass production, where a certain number had to be made because you knew that some hefty percentage would be bad. The cost of that is enormous. As much as 25 percent of a manufacturing plant's budget is spent to find and fix mistakes. Where the concentration is on continual improvement, the plant gets greater production at less cost. Deming's comment on this point was "What people need is leadership and help, not just to be required to turn out so many. That will not bring improvement. That will not decrease costs."

• • •

12. Remove Barriers to Joy in Work

"This will mean," Deming said, "abolish the annual rating or merit system which ranks people, creates competition, conflict." Annual ratings of personnel were initially designed to solve a problem. Companies had to find out who was doing well and should be rewarded and who was doing so poorly that he or she should be replaced. An annual personal rating, it was initially believed, was a systematic and objective way to find out. Actually, it is not at all systematic, it is anything but objective, and it answers neither question. What it does do is enormous harm. Norb Keller at General Motors explains it well. "What gives me the right," he asks, "to tell you that you're in the lower 25 percent? Does that make you feel good? Does that make you think you're going to do it better in the future? I think probably it just makes you feel bad, and you'd want to do something else."

Keep in mind that two-thirds of the people in any group are not in the upper third and that roughly half of them are below average. Half of them are definitely below the median. After studying the Deming management system, the Department of the Navy stopped forcing its best people to compete for ratings. The Navy realized that it was eliminating or discouraging about half of its best personnel.

The annual rating and merit system does to people exactly what competition does to departments (point 9)—it forces them to compete no matter what. You cannot take joy or pride in your work if your main goal is to beat someone else to get some sort of external reward. You know this already: The only lifelong, reliable motivations are those that come from within, and one of the strongest of those is the joy and pride that grow from knowing that you've just done something as well as you can do it. Conversely, if a person is made to feel unimportant or inadequate, the only reason he'll work at all is for the money, an external and inadequate motivation. Deming liked to tell the story of the habitually absent worker whose boss demanded to know why he worked only four days of a five-day week. "Because," the worker answered, "I can't get by on what you pay me for three days." Remember the comparative absentee rates in Great Britain that we mentioned in the Introduction that seem to indicate that workers in a quality management system are absent 40 percent less than workers in traditional systems.

The object of removing all the barriers is to let people take pride and joy in their work, rather than in their rating.

As a practical matter, people want to know how they are doing, and their manager wants to know as well. Rather than a rating, some companies now call each worker in at least once a year for a long chat on how each feels about the company and his or her place in it, and each worker is always asked how the manager can make it easier for him or her to do the work. There is no rating, no comparison; there is an honest assessment on both sides of what is happening and what needs to happen.

◆ ◆ ◆

13. Institute Education and Self-Improvement

Do not confuse education with training (point 6). Training is for the specific skills that you need to do a specific job and other skills that you would need to do any job. Education has to do with—to quote Deming—"anything whatever to keep people's minds developing." When we talk about continual improvement of the system, there is a tendency to forget that the people in the organization are also critical parts of the system and must themselves be continually improved. Nothing in life is static; it either gets better, or it gets worse. That includes people, so while training for skills is finished when the skill is learned, education is never finished.

One of the difficulties with education in the United States at all levels is that we have been led to believe that if we get a diploma or a degree or a certificate of some sort, that is all we need, an achievement to last a lifetime. It is not, nor could it be. Too many things change too rapidly for any education, no matter how high the level, to be adequate to our personal, corporate, and national needs. "No organization," Deming said, "can survive with just good people. They need people that are improving."

• • •

14. Accomplish the Transformation

Knowing all that you now know does you no good at all if you do not put it to use. To put it to use, you must not only believe that the Deming quality management system will work, you must develop a "critical mass" of associates who also believe it will work. What you are searching for is co-operation, everyone using what they know to accomplish the aim of the organization. What they must believe, and what must in fact be true, is that if the organization wins, everybody wins. That is the point of cooperation instead of competition—win-win rewards everyone; win-lose seems to reward some and punish others, but in the long run everyone is punished by losing internal motivation.

While everyone needs to know the 14 Points, the truth is that getting a quality management system going depends on top management. "Quality goes all the way through an organization," Deming said, "but it can be no better than the intent of the top people." It is possible, however, for employees below that level to influence top management, to suggest that there might be a better way, that Deming was right when he said, "With better quality and lower costs, you can capture the market." We do not pretend that achieving that sort of influence is easy, but it is possible. Think of it as psychological warfare at the cor-porate level, and never forget that subtlety counts. As Grandmother used to say, "You can catch more flies with honey than you can with vinegar." It's amazing how many of those silly-sounding bromides that you shrug off as a child turn out to be true.

Well done, Granny!

5

* * * * *

Zytec and Wallace

He was a bold man that first eat an oyster.
—Jonathan Swift

Early in the 1980s, the Control Data Corporation, one of the electronics industry giants, decided that it should not be in businesses that were not part of its basic strength. With three other firms, Control Data owned a company that made power supply units, electronic devices that convert regular household current (AC) supplied by a local utility to the highly regulated direct current (DC) that computers, telecommunications equipment, and medical devices need. The smaller ones are the size of a pocket calculator and weigh two pounds; the larger ones weigh two hundred pounds and are the size of two VCRs stacked. An executive of Control Data asked Ronald D. Schmidt, a mid-level manager there, if he wanted to put together a group to buy the power supply plant in Redwood Falls, Minnesota, and become an independent company, an outside supplier to Control Data, rather than remain a part of the parent company.

Schmidt's initial reaction was "Hell, no." The more he thought of it, however, the more it appealed to him as a new challenge. He approached John Steel and Larry Matthews, colleagues at Control Data who had talents he did not have—respectively, marketing and engineering.

Steel remembers having two thoughts when Schmidt approached him: "What the heck is a power supply, and where the heck is Redwood Falls?" His third thought was "Can we make it on our own without billions of Control Data dollars protecting us?" The three of them decided to give it a try if they could find the financing to put the deal together.

In 1983, there was plenty of money to finance leveraged buyouts. As Schmidt says, "This was before LBO became a four-letter word!" Wall Street would go on to make buyouts an everyone-can-play, big-money sport. In 1984, the power supply division of Control Data became Zytec Corporation, with headquarters in Bloomington, Minnesota. (It has since moved to Eden Prairie.) That factual recitation is misleading; nothing ever goes that smoothly. "It cost us twice as much time," Steel says, "and twice as much money as we had originally expected." That is a bit of hyperbole. It did take twice as much time—eleven months instead of five—but the purchase price was more or less what Schmidt expected—$5 million.

The company name, Zytec, doesn't mean anything. Schmidt says he made up the name because he wanted "a two-syllable, harsh, powerful-sounding, memorable name that no one else was using." It has no other meaning. "Tec" does stand for technology, but "zy" is only the last two letters of the alphabet backwards and means nothing.

Schmidt heads the company, with Steel as vice president of marketing and sales. Matthews was head of engineering until he retired in April 1993. Employees sometimes refer to them as "the founders." They never thought of themselves that way. The company already existed; they changed its form, but not its business and not, in the beginning, its main customer. In the early days, Control Data was its biggest client. That is no longer true and hasn't been for some time. By 1990, Zytec had grown to the point that Control Data accounted for less than 2 percent of Zytec's revenue and was only one of twenty customer companies. What had attracted the new customers was quality.

When Zytec was created, Schmidt, Steel, and Matthews already knew from research that product quality in the power supply industry was, at best, mediocre. If Zytec could become a highly reliable quality company, it could stand out in the industry and do well. "We knew we had to change," Schmidt says, "but we didn't know exactly what to do." Steel had attended a seminar on quality given at Control Data by Dr. Deming. Schmidt and Steel reviewed a copy of Deming's book *Out of the Crisis* and decided to take it to the first long-range planning meeting with senior managers in July 1984. They knew that Deming was given the credit for the success of Japanese companies, so "we just decided we'd take a leap of faith." Schmidt says to try to compare Zytec before Deming and Zytec after Deming is like taking your kids to see Grandma after a year, and she immediately says, "My God, they've grown a foot!" You see them every day, and to you they don't appear to have grown at all. "It's really difficult for me to talk about it," he says, "because it has been an evolutionary process." He says that after a sudden and sharp drop in business in 1985, "all the employees knew we had to change."

It would have been impossible not to know. "In 1984 and 1985, we were shipping late, if we shipped at all," Steel remembers, "and when we shipped the product, the customer was dissatisfied with the quality that we were shipping." Of every one hundred power supply units built, five to ten had faults that had to be reworked before they could be shipped. "We were uncompetitive back in 1984," Schmidt says. "That's why we went to a commitment to Deming to begin with, because we knew we had to change. We had to increase the quality level of our products; we had to bring the cost of our products down."

The problem was not the people at Zytec, but the way the plant was organized, the company's management system. Like most other American manufacturers, Zytec used the "scientific" organization of the factory, suggested by Frederick W. Taylor in 1911, and the business organization introduced by Alfred Sloan at GM in the 1920s. "If we were following either of those fundamentals [Taylor or Sloan] in 1992," Steel says, "we would not be in existence today."

Pat O'Malley, a unit manager who came up through the ranks, says everything was rigid in the old days, with specific rules that you followed mindlessly, no matter what. "Not a lot was expected of each individual," she says. "It was the old hang your brain at the door, come do what you're told, and go home." She agrees with Steel: "We wouldn't be in business today if we did business like we used to." Dale Janssen, a senior engineer with Zytec and Control Data for almost thirty years, remembers that the whole system relied on inspection, and "it was very, very costly. . . . We had problems with almost every product."

Starting in 1984, small groups of Zytec people began to attend Deming's four-day seminars. Douglas Tersteeg, now director of the quality department, went in 1984 and still remembers the Red Bead Experiment. As a reminder, it demonstrates that if the system is not organized to produce quality, no matter what the employees do, no matter how hard they work, no matter how much they want to succeed, they cannot produce consistent quality, and inspecting what they turn out will not improve it. All inspection can do is catch mistakes that have already been made. In 1984, Zytec had thirty-four inspectors in the quality department. By mid-1985, those inspectors were transferred into manufacturing positions. "That was a major milestone in our journey toward implementing Deming's 14 Points," Tersteeg says.

Milestones are rarely easy. "Finding a place to start, I think, was very, very difficult," Janssen says. "We didn't know what to do first." Vickie Martin, a sales representative, was on one of three teams set up to see how the 14 Points applied to Zytec. "We must have spent between six and twelve months," she remembers, "just coming to some consensus in our own groups as to what the points we were assigned meant." Getting started was only part of the problem. "It wasn't an easy change," O'Malley says. "From one day to the next, we were in constant turmoil."

Of the 14 Points, Schmidt says, "Some of them are just common sense and make a lot of sense. Some of them, whoo!" It is the usual reaction from executives who have been successful with standard American management techniques. "If you start to read and understand what Dr. Deming is saying," Steel says, "the first thing you have to do is 'tape erase' a lot of the things that you were taught, and learned, and applied in your previous business life." Two techniques that were popular in the mid-1980s—pay for performance and management by objective—had to be erased at Zytec.

Of the first, the Deming management system insists that merit pay and performance appraisals are wrong; therefore, pay for performance is out. If a person can only produce what the system allows—good or bad—why should the person be punished if it's bad or rewarded if it's good? More important, if workers are individually rewarded, why should they cooperate with each other? Since cooperation is the key to successful quality, anything that interferes with cooperation is wrong.

The second popular technique in 1984, management by objective, sounds like a good idea. The boss says to a subordinate, "I don't care how you do it, just get it done!" For the subordinate, it could be an opportunity to show his ability, and if he's lucky, it is. If, however, he's not lucky, and the job is not getting done, he might be tempted to do anything, no matter what. Better to cut corners than to fail, because what the boss has actually said is "The end justifies the means," which is always unethical, sometimes immoral, and occasionally criminal (to use consultant Brian Joiner's three levels of questionable conduct). Since we have never found a quality company that was not also an ethical company, management by objective won't do.

The Deming method also urges quality companies to have single sources of supply for whatever they buy, and to help those suppliers improve their own quality so that they can produce better products for less cost. (Zytec is itself the single supplier for eighteen of its twenty clients.) Before introducing the Deming quality management system, Schmidt had always had multiple suppliers for everything. Now he had to have single suppliers and trust them. "Completely, a hundred eighty degrees contrary to everything we'd grown up doing," he says. Matthews, with his engineering background, says of single-source supplying, "I've believed that for years." Engineers understand reliability; executives understand supply costs. In fact at

Zytec, Matthews may have been the executive who had the least trouble adapting. "Deming made sense," he says. "If you read through the principles, they really make sense to me, each one of them."

If Deming is easier for engineers, his system is harder for middle managers and line supervisors. "The middle managers," Tersteeg says, "are the ones that seem to have the most difficulty in accepting this change to empowering the work force because they view it as an erosion of their authority." It is not only an erosion of their authority, it is a total change in how management functions and what its job is. Managers have to be taught the new management system. "We developed our own course on our culture," Schmidt says, "to tell people why we were changing, and how they were going to change, and give them some tools to deal with making change, because change is difficult for every one of us. . . . We tried to tell them why change was difficult, and it's all right to have this difficulty."

Managers, Schmidt knew, were supposed to be controllers, but now Deming insisted that they be coaches and give up control. That point was easier for Schmidt to understand than for some others. "I was always pretty big on trusting employees. I trust you until I find out that I can't, but that's not the way a lot of companies operate." That trust made it easier for him to give the employees more authority, but it did not make it any easier for middle managers, and Schmidt knew that. "Particularly a first-line manager in manufacturing," he says. "Their whole lives they were trained to go beat up on people—'Don't give me excuses, get it done!' and 'Just go out there and make it happen!' And then you come along and say, 'Oh, you're going to be a coach now. You know, you've got to coach your people.' Tough transition, a very tough transition to make."

"You start to understand," Steel says, "that Dr. Deming's challenge to us was to open ourselves up, to trust the employees, to delegate, to get out of their way instead of trying to micromanage them, to lead instead of trying to direct their every behavior, to give them the tools to do the job." O'Malley, the former worker turned manager, says things changed after Deming: "Everybody had a say in what was going on, you know? We were asked our opinions. Our opinions counted. We were listened to." Which was a new experience for Mary Moudry, an assembler with fifteen years at Zytec. "Where before," she says, "they would be right on us telling us what we were doing wrong, and how we were doing it, and how we should have been doing it."

Tersteeg now insists, "If you want quality, you've got to put it into the hands of the people who are closest to the process." The people at Zytec understand that. "I understand what Deming was trying to accomplish," Robin Stegner, a manager, says, "when he was describing that people need to be leaders of teams, rather than supervisors of employees." Zytec is Stegner's first job in management, and she believes the Deming method makes it easier for her. "What Deming tells you," she says, "is to ask the people doing the job because they're the ones who know the most about it . . . there is a lot of pressure removed because you don't always have to be the one to come up with the best way, or the right way, or the most efficient way. You can look to your team to help you do that." Schmidt, who has years of management experience, sees the same benefit. "The problem with the old way," he says, "is you had to be smart enough to have all the answers, and I never was smart enough to have all the answers." From the beginning, he was willing to listen to the people on the line and to promote them.

"At the time I attended the Deming seminar," O'Malley says, "I was only in management for a year, and I had worked my way up through the ranks, so it made common sense to me. I didn't have years of management experience saying, 'Can we or can't we do this?' Deming was speaking the way a line person would speak. Give me an opportunity to fix what my problem is rather than have people far removed from the problem assume that they knew exactly what the problem was, and they could fix it."

The change at Zytec is not simply a matter of letting the people who do the work actually do it; it is more basic than that. It is a matter of broad trust. "We're on a trust roll at Zytec," Steel says. "We have done so many things based on trust, trusting everybody to work forty hours a week without time cards or time clocks." The trust even extends to financial figures, which most private companies keep completely secret. "We've always shown our employees our financial results," Schmidt says. "We're a private company, and that's pretty unusual for a private company, but we've always done that. We've always tried to give as much information as we can to our employees, because we believe if they understand what it is we're trying to do, they can buy in much easier."

To adopt the Deming quality management system requires that you rethink the relative value of management and labor, particularly in the assignment of blame. Until the early 1980s, it was common for American industrial managers to blame anything that went wrong on labor. General Motors spent $80 billion on technology because senior executives were convinced that workers were responsible for quality problems, and those problems would go away if technology replaced people. It didn't work, and GM had to start all over again. Deming would not tolerate blaming the worker. Martin, the Zytec sales rep, says, "The lasting impression that I got from our meeting with Dr. Deming is what a valiant supporter of the little people, the nonmanagement people, he is." He was also a critic of management, as Steel noticed. "He has laid this incredible guilt trip on American business and industry," he says, "with his perception that if something is going wrong with the products or the processes, management is somewhere between 85 and 94 percent to blame. And to those of us in management who were omnipotent in our wisdom and pure in our direction during the sixties and seventies, this was hard to understand, but you have to [understand it] for survival."

All employees at Zytec are trained, and for manufacturing employees, compensation is based on how many different jobs each can do. "Without training," Tersteeg says, "you can't have quality." Without training, Schmidt says, you can't convince anyone that you mean what you say about quality. "We did a lot of training," he says. "We had to give them the tools, whether that be skills, or knowledge, or equipment, or whatever. Once we did that, and they really took us seriously and trusted us, they stepped forward very, very well." Stegner, the material control manager, says it isn't just training, it's how you train. She was at a Deming seminar when she realized that training employees by putting them "under somebody else's wing" won't work. She says that to have "sequential employee training"—A trains B, B trains C, C trains D, and D trains E, which is fairly typical in industry—"by the time it gets to E, they don't understand why they're doing what they're doing." No one can do a job correctly if he or she does not know why that job is being done. "And that really turned on light bulbs for a lot of us in the seminar," Stegner says.

Light bulbs do not all go on simultaneously. Even if the workers on the line were going to benefit in the long run, there was a natural suspicion among the workers that existed in the beginning. Years of adversarial relations do not instantly disappear because a new program starts. Mary Moudry remembers the beginning. "They put up a big sign saying, SIGN UP FOR THIS [QUALITY PROGRAM] IF YOU WANT TO BE INVOLVED. Well, we, none of us, wanted to be involved because we didn't know what it was. It was like eating oyster stew the first time. You don't know for sure if you're going to like it or not, and we didn't even want to try it."

What often prevents people from wanting to try is the fear of what will happen if they or the program should fail. The fear of change, the fear of failure, are natural parts of the human psyche. Knowing that, management has to find a way to control that fear, to keep it within some bounds that will not interfere with a quality system. Fear exists in places you would not expect, and at Zytec, the best place to illustrate that is in the sales department, where all sales people are now on salary. There are no more sales commissions.

Paul Pasqua is the national sales manager. "There was a certain amount of fear [under the commission system] that the sales people had," he says, "that if they didn't sell, then they would not make the money. They might not be able to make their house payment, or their car payment, or not continue to live the life-style they were accustomed to. Or the fear of going home and telling your wife or husband, 'We're not making the money this month we thought we were,' the embarrassment that would have. They're less fearful now."

Vickie Martin, the sales rep, says, "Eliminating incentive pay was a great release to me. . . . I'm able to stay forward-focused on bigger issues and make sure that my customer is well served at all times." Paychecks become predictable, and as Pasqua says, "Maybe they don't have the peaks, but they also don't have the valleys." As the sales manager, he thinks it's wonderful. "We're able to put two sales people on an account," he says, "and they're not worried about who landed what first, or who did the most work, or things like that." It is Deming's point about the importance of cooperation: If you don't have it, you can't have quality. "[The sales people] really want to be part of a team," Pasqua says, "they enjoy being part of a team. If they didn't, they really wouldn't be at Zytec now."

There is another benefit for Zytec. Since there are no commissions and no quotas in sales, Pasqua says, "No salesperson [has] an incentive to 'sandbag' or lie about the orders that are coming down the pike, and therefore our whole forecasting system works better."

There were plenty of successes. Under the old management system, if parts came in that were rejected, whoever inspected and rejected them had to fill out a twenty-six-page form with 260 questions, and then get five signatures from five departments before the rejected material could be returned to the supplier. After studying the Deming management system, Zytec had its first major reorganization and discovered in 1985 that it had half a million dollars' worth of rejected parts stacked in the warehouse. By using statistical process control to find out what was going on, employees got control of the warehouse. "We went from half a million dollars of material that was defective," Tersteeg says, "and a cycle time of fifty days to get it sent back, to under $5,000 and a cycle time of one day." The warehouse now functions so well that auditors no longer require a physical inventory at year's end. It is the sort of breakthrough improvement that is the stuff of management dreams.

Cycle time for design and for manufacturing has been cut in half, and cycle time has been cut nearly in half in hiring new employees. "You don't just focus on manufacturing," Schmidt says; "you focus on improving your total company."

It was in the sales department that the quality effort at Zytec expanded from a manufacturing effort to a total effort. The cycle time in manufacturing to make one product had been cut from thirteen days to three days. "The vice president of manufacturing pointed out to me," Steel says, "using data, that it was now taking me seven days to get the order from the customer into his plant." In other words, it took more than twice as long to get the order into the plant as it took to build the device and ship it out. "That was one of those 'Aha!' moments for me," Steel says. The tools that applied in manufacturing should also apply in marketing, sales, engineering—everywhere. "Together we could be on this quality crusade rather than it just being a *manufacturing* quality crusade."

Using the tools, particularly statistics, also changed the way people could discuss problems. Schmidt remembers the meeting when he learned how much that could mean. "Our controller, who was a reasonably confrontational person, said in one of our meetings, 'You know what I like about statistical process control? It takes the personality out of the discussion.' And, God, that really hit me! If you can get the personality out of it, then you get it on the table, and you deal with it. But if it's a personal attack on me, then, boy, 'To hell with you!' " When the head of manufacturing told the head of sales that sales orders were taking too long to get to the plant, he did it "using data." It was not a personal attack. It was a presentation of statistical information, no more personal or threatening than the odds on improving a hand in draw poker.

Other improvements sound modest on paper but made an enormous difference to the people doing the work. The warehouse was so dimly lit that one employee would crawl around with a cigarette lighter to read part numbers on boxes on the bottom shelf. It had always been like that. "Everyone had just kind of assumed," Stegner says, "that's the way it was. It took one of the employees to say, 'It doesn't need to be this way; we can make an improvement.' " Without a quality program, it is doubtful that any employee would have felt secure enough to make the suggestion—clearly, none had for years—and had some worker had the courage to make the suggestion, it is doubtful that management would have paid any attention. The gain for Zytec was not only better lighting and a more efficient warehouse, but proof of a more cooperative, less fearful work force.

"One of the real upsides to continuous improvement at Zytec," Stegner says, "is that if you try something, and you outgrow it, you're never penalized for that." She remembers a sequential numbering machine bought for about three hundred dollars to make the warehouse more efficient. "Well, within six weeks of buying the machine," she says, "we figured out a better process where we didn't need the machine. In another company, people might have accused the warehouse manager of poor judgment in investing three hundred dollars in a machine he only used for six weeks, but at Zytec, we all said, 'Isn't it terrific that in only six weeks they figured out a way to eliminate that step in their process.' "

There are also downsides to continual improvement. "I always say that the flip side of continuous improvement," Stegner says, "is the implication that you're not good enough." Steel refers to it as "exhausting" and "a never-ending race." He adds, "Those of us who like to see things wrapped in nice, neat little packages, and a finish line, and a victory stand, and nirvana achieved, have to understand that that will never happen." The customers are the reason for continual improvement. "Things can't stay the same," Martin of sales says. "Expectations are always being ratcheted up. You have to constantly meet higher and higher demands. It's a necessary part of doing business."

Mary Moudry, she of the oyster stew, thinks that the Deming management system has changed things for the people on the factory floor: "I think people listen to each other more. Managers listen to the floor people, and floor people are even listening back and forth to each other and to the manager. I think there's more teamwork, definitely more teamwork." Another change is that the bosses tend to give them more leeway, "and sometimes we find better ways from what they were doing before." What she likes best is the way relationships have changed, how she now feels more like part of the company. "We never felt like anybody cared about us before," she says.

If that sounds warm and fuzzy, and what is wanted are dollars-and-cents results, try these figures: In 1991, during a recession, Zytec's revenue grew by 28 percent. The company's revenue per employee was $110,000, well above the industry average. Since 1988, scrap and rework have been cut 66 percent, warranty costs have fallen by 72 percent, and productivity improvement rose 75 percent. Cycle times in design and manufacturing have been cut. On-time delivery of all products exceeds 95 percent, and product costs have been reduced 30 to 40 percent.

Zytec is moving toward Six Sigma quality, the standard adopted and defined by Motorola. To round off the math a little, Six Sigma requires fewer than 4 mistakes per million. On some products—not all—Zytec is already there well ahead of its own demanding schedule. (As a comparison, most United States firms usually operate at from 4,000 to 6,000 mistakes per million—some are as high as 60,000—and Japanese auto supply firms are usually at about 1,000.)

In 1992, *Industry Week* magazine said the Zytec plant in Redwood Falls was one of the ten best factories in the nation. Zytec does not publicly disclose earnings, but it was profitable in 1990 and 1991 on revenues of about $56 million and $79 million, respectively. And of those employees who never before felt that anyone cared about them? In 1992, the 494 employees made on average 4.4 quality-improvement suggestions each, every one of which was adopted. "The more brains you get into a program," engineer Matthews says, "and the more cooperation and people thinking about it, the better. . . . I've thought for years, how do you really get people involved? I think that's where I'm impressed with the Deming principles. It really gives you sort of a method of getting people involved." If we have learned anything about quality, it is this: If there is no worker involvement, there is no quality system.

Not only are Zytec's workers involved, some of their children are as well. The company's 1993 calendar, sent to employees and customers, featured reproductions of fourteen crayon pictures drawn by children of their parents at work in the company. Other pictures, drawn by 180 employee children, decorate the lobbies of company buildings. Steel says Zytec can't match the huge lobbies and expensive artwork favored by major corporations, so "we did the next-best thing."

Continual improvement goes on. Schmidt says, "You need to understand that we still struggle with this. . . . It's not for the faint of heart because, boy, there are a lot of detours and stumbling along the way. You've got to commit yourself to change and just keep plugging away at it day after day after day." He says that quality improvement under Deming "is a way of life!" Asked if in the beginning he found it difficult to change, Steel replies, "Not only did I initially find it difficult to change, I find it continuing to be difficult to change." If it is difficult, it is also exciting. "I feel there are still so many things left to do," Stegner says, "that I can imagine myself in this department for many years to come without getting bored with my job." Melody Mork is one of the last people to see Zytec products before they leave the plant. She packages them. Continual improvement makes sense to her. "Nobody's perfect," she says, "we've got to keep going . . . better and better."

What is critical to remember is the reason any company would start a quality management system. The object of the exercise is business success achieved by producing higher-quality goods at lower costs and creating more jobs, thereby helping the economy whether you meant to or not. Zytec, for instance, used to have its printed circuit boards made inexpensively in Mexico. From the time Zytec got the materials together and shipped the kit to Mexico until the time the circuit boards came back, were installed, and shipped to waiting customers, eighty-two days had passed. The same work is now done in Minnesota in four days. Higher quality, lower costs, a cycle time of one-twentieth what it used to be, and a return of manufacturing jobs to the United States. Award-winning performance by an award-winning company.

Zytec first applied for the Malcolm Baldrige National Quality Award in 1990, made it to the final fifteen companies in the manufacturing category, but did not win. Ronald D. Schmidt, the CEO, had wanted to try two years earlier. "Back in 'eighty-eight," he says, "I was looking for something to get a little more excitement into the company rather than just talk about Deming's concepts." He looked at the Baldrige criteria and asked his management staff what they thought. They thought not. " 'We have too much on our plate,' basically, was what came back," he says. Douglas Tersteeg of the quality department remembers that his advice was "Let's get the ship on course here so we're not headed for the reef, and then we'll consider the Baldrige."

The next year, Schmidt studied the Baldrige criteria, comparing the requirements with Deming's 14 Points to see if they were compatible. "The last thing I want to do is confuse people with something that I think is contradictory to what we've been trying to do for all these years." He concluded that people would not be confused using Deming's management system to complete the Baldrige application. They decided to go ahead. "We looked at it for two years," Tersteeg says, "before we finally said, 'I think we can do it now.'" Senior managers decided in 1989 to apply the next year. When they didn't win, they decided to try again right away.

By studying the 1990 Baldrige evaluation and working on the company's weaker areas, Zytec won the Baldrige Award in 1991. Melody Mork, the packer, remembers how she felt when she learned Zytec had won the Malcolm Baldrige National Quality Award: "Hallelujah, we done something good!" Pat O'Malley says, "I think we all felt the sense of being one big team." And Robin Stegner saw a personal value. "We all knew there would be some publicity and lots of visitors," she remembers, "but to many of us, it was a much more personal validation that all of this hard work is paying off for us."

There are also solid business benefits. "Winning the Baldrige has been a tremendous aid in selling," Paul Pasqua reports. "It immediately gives you a tremendous amount of credibility in the call [on a potential customer]. It makes you, even if you've never shipped them a product, you're a high-quality supplier automatically." Winning the Baldrige Award, says John Steel of marketing, "makes it very easy for those customers to put the next product, and the next product, and the next product into Zytec. And make no mistake about it, we have incredible competition out there in the marketplace."

Pasqua even sees a benefit for early customers, the people who gave them business four or five years ago, before they won anything. "Now they look like geniuses back inside their companies," he says, "and we've made them feel real good about choosing us." People who feel good about choosing a company will not leave that company lightly.

Larry Matthews, the engineer, credits the Deming

management system for the Baldrige Award. "I think that's what really helped in winning the Baldrige, the fact that we were using the Deming principles, and we could put that down on paper and demonstrate [that] we had the process." Deming would probably have been happier without the credit. He was opposed to the Baldrige Award and had been from the first proposal. Invited to testify about the possibility of establishing an award by a congressional subcommittee, Deming declined to appear, as a demonstration of his opposition to it. The people at Zytec who successfully used his philosophy to win the award do not understand his opposition.

"I look at Baldrige and Deming as two different things," Schmidt says. "Deming's philosophy is a road map to a transformation. Baldrige, to me, is a wayside stop on the transformation, and the criteria measure you and say how you are doing. . . . I don't see a conflict." He says Baldrige is nothing more than an audit. Dale Janssen, the longtime engineer, says, "I think the Deming philosophy is a method of operating . . . and I think the Baldrige is a way of checking that you did do what you thought you wanted to do." On the factory floor, Baldrige criteria were used to check processes, and employees would discover omissions or operating glitches that they hadn't noticed before. "If you look at the Baldrige as a growth opportunity," Janssen says, "or a check opportunity, it can really help you."

Tersteeg says, "I understand Dr. Deming has some problems with the Baldrige Award in that it tries to rate or quantify amounts of training, the effectiveness of it. I think that's a misinterpretation." He says since the criteria do not tell you what to do, the key is to interpret the criteria within the Deming philosophy. If you do that,

"Baldrige goes hand in glove with the fourteen management principles."

Steel, the head of marketing, says what they learned from Deming let Zytec win the Baldrige Award. "The gifts that Dr. Deming gave us," he says, "with the value system and his 14 Points . . . and the gifts that he gave us with specific statistical process control were the platform, the foundation, upon which we were able to answer the very insightful Baldrige questions with some extremely good answers, and demonstrated improvement, and demonstrated increased customer satisfaction." Steel not only doesn't see any conflict between Deming and Baldrige, he doesn't think the point is worth raising and certainly is not worth arguing. "There are always people who would like to drag you into Deming versus Baldrige, or Deming versus Juran, or Juran versus Crosby, and I think that's such an incredible waste of time," he says. "Those of us who are running the race are too busy running the race to spend a lot of time dissecting the minute differences between Deming, Baldrige, Juran, Crosby, etc." *

To Deming, the differences were anything but minute. Informed of the "wayside stop" comparison, he said to Schmidt, "It's nothing of the kind; it's not that at all." His complaint was that companies are using the Baldrige criteria as a method to achieve quality, which, everyone at Zytec would agree, is a bad idea. The Baldrige criteria measure quality, and knowing how to use a tape measure or a T square doesn't make you a carpenter. Measurement

* * * * * * * * * *

* The reference is to Dr. Joseph Juran in Connecticut and Philip Crosby in Florida, both well-known quality authorities.

can only tell you how much or how many; it cannot tell you how or why.

At Zytec, Baldrige and Deming are different chapters from the same book of quality production. From the chief executive to line workers, people speak easily of using one or more of the 14 Points to fill in the seven sections of the Baldrige application. Tersteeg says, "Frankly, I'm puzzled at why Dr. Deming has not embraced the [Baldrige] process more readily." Or even at all. "They go hand in hand," O'Malley says. "They mesh together. I didn't see that we had to do anything special to win the Baldrige. . . . It would be kind of like if you had a classic car, and you wanted to enter it in a contest. You'd polish it up and shine it, and then you'd go out and win the contest. We kind of put a spit shine on what we were doing."

Tersteeg and others at Zytec say that the American quality experts are all "preaching the same gospel" and which one you adopt is less important than your dedication and commitment to quality. "When you boil it all down," he says, "there are just two basic principles at the heart of all this. One is the Golden Rule that we all learned back in kindergarten—'Do unto others as you would have them do unto you'—and the other is 'When I get up tomorrow morning, I'm going to do things better than I did them yesterday.' "

Wanting to do better is important. Knowing how to do better is critical. As Deming so often asked, "By what method?"

Zytec did not set out to win the Malcolm Baldrige National Quality Award. Zytec employees, all of them, had been working on a quality program for almost seven years, starting when upper managers went through Deming's book in July 1984. They knew they had to change. "I'm thoroughly convinced," Schmidt says, "[that] if you want to have an organization rise up the heights, you can't do it the old way." The question remains: How?

"Take the Deming points," Matthews says, "break those up into various categories like we did and . . . get all levels of people involved in the company working with those points. Don't try to do it yourself, but get the full spectrum of people down to the direct-line people all the way through the organization. Set up teams to work in implementing the points so you get their thoughts and get them behind it." Martin of sales suggests that you expect a lot; small changes aren't much help. Most of all, she says, "Listen to everyone. Listen well to your customers, listen well to your coworkers and all employees, and use every opportunity to understand where improvements can be made."

Mary Moudry, a line worker, says you have to be ready to accept criticism and to give it, and "learn to be a team member." Melody Mork thinks that's the key. "If nobody is part of a team with me," she says, "I won't get my job done, and they won't get their job done if I don't help out."

"You have to get everybody committed," Schmidt says, "and everybody using their knowledge as opposed to just a few people telling [all the other] people what to do." O'Malley, who worked her way up, may feel the labor-management changes more keenly. "As far as the roles of management changing, I think we've become more leaders and coaches, and the whole effort is more of a team effort. We all get involved in that, and it's a good feeling. You walk away feeling that a group of people have accomplished something. It's a real win-win situation, rather than a win-lose situation of the past."

The Deming quality management system was successfully installed at Zytec for a number of reasons. Ronald D. Schmidt, John Steel, and Larry Matthews knew that Zytec Corporation (the system) was not doing well in the electronics industry (the expanded system), but they had a specific plan (vision) to change that: Produce the best-quality power supply on the market to ensure a future for the company and its people. They were able to explain that plan (communicate that vision) to their employees and to convince the employees that they meant it. To do that, they employed Deming's 14 Points and created an atmosphere in which people were willing to take risks, make suggestions, and continually improve. That requires an atmosphere of cooperation, not competition; an atmosphere of teamwork and shared goals, not individual effort for personal gain.

The most important change that adoption of a quality management system requires cannot even be seen; it requires a change in attitude by senior management, middle management and supervisors, and workers, and the attitude that needs to be changed is different for each group. For example, senior managers must accept that they cannot possibly know everything that needs to be known, and workers have to accept that they cannot rely on senior managers to make all the suggestions and decisions; and the workers must contribute not only with their job skills but with their knowledge as well. Their outdated beliefs have to be changed, and everyone has to learn to control fear. That requires training, and the training has to be done under the guidance of Profound Knowledge.

Zytec had to change or go out of business, but it could not close temporarily and make the changes that were needed to stay in business. Power supply units had to be made and shipped even while personnel were being trained in ways to make them better. The warehouse may have been a huge mess, but supplies had to be ordered and processed. Zytec had to continue to perform as it had in the past while it worked desperately to change for the future. It was not neat and tidy.

It was, however, successful. Any other way of which we are aware would have involved unacceptable risks.

◆   ◆   ◆   ◆   ◆

The obituary was on page 81 of the *Oil & Gas Journal* on March 1, 1993. It announced that Wilson Industries, Inc., of Houston, Texas, "has acquired the operating assets of Wallace Co., Inc." Wallace had won the Malcolm Baldrige National Quality Award in October 1990, enjoyed its fifteen months of fame, then filed for bankruptcy in January 1992. Wallace was the first distribution company and only the second small business to win the Baldrige Award. Winning the award has been blamed, at least in part, for the financial collapse of the family-owned, Houston-based business. We do not believe that is true.

The Wallace Company filed for Chapter 11 bankruptcy protection in a federal court in Corpus Christi, Texas, about 180 miles south of Houston, and apparently only a few people in the city were aware of the filing until four days later when the *Houston Chronicle* reported it on the paper's first business page. The article said that after winning the Baldrige Award "company officers began leading tour after tour through its offices and were big draws on the lecture circuit. . . . The tours, speeches, and interviews kept company officers from turning the already troubled company around."

A business news wire story that day led its report

with its opinion: "Too bad officials at Wallace Co. forgot one thing after winning the coveted Malcolm Baldrige National Quality Award. Mainly how to run a profitable business." (The report was reprinted in at least two major city daily newspapers, and both corrected the punctuation.) Chairman John Wallace admitted that he and others were distracted by the award. "You really get caught up in the euphoria," he said. "You want to help everyone else out. It was our own fault. My fault." Gail Cooper of the Cooper Group in Dallas, hired to save the company, said, "The company had officials that just let it get out of hand. They got so wrapped up in the award."

The implication was that officials were celebrating winning the Baldrige Award, and quality killed the company. None of the reports about the bankruptcy we've seen pointed out that one requirement of the Baldrige Award is that companies that win must share information on what they did with anyone who asks. Obviously, that is less demanding on larger companies than it is on smaller ones, but we wonder what part quality actually played in the company's failure. Only two weeks before he filed for bankruptcy protection, John Wallace defended the company's quality program, saying that without it, the company would have been driven out of business years earlier. On the evidence, that is probably true.

The Wallace Company was founded in 1942 by C. S. Wallace, Sr., and the year it won the Baldrige Award, it had ten offices in Texas, Louisiana, and Alabama. It distributed pipes, valves, fittings, and specialty products in the oil and chemical businesses. The company had done reasonably well until the mid-1980s, when Murphy's Law took over with a vengeance: Everything that could go wrong in the economy along the Gulf Coast went wrong. Almost all of it was beyond the company's control.

Domestic steel pipe producers, led by U.S. Steel, cut prices, making Wallace's inventory much less valuable. The Gulf Coast oil industry had gone sour, eventually causing a regional economic crash, helped along by the savings and loan scandal that had hit Texas particularly hard. The bank Wallace had done business with had its own problems and canceled the company's $15 million revolving line of credit. As a supplier in the petrochemical industry, Wallace was hurt by the Persian Gulf War. Refiners stopped investing in capital improvements, so orders to suppliers dried up, and some of them sold their inventories for ten cents on the dollar. Companies all over Texas were suffering, and some of them were turning to quality programs to help them survive. Hoechst Celanese Corporation told Wallace that in the future it would buy only from suppliers with quality programs. "We really had no other choice," Wallace said. "We didn't get into the quality movement to win an award, as our critics have charged. We did it to set ourselves apart from the competition."

It was the same reason that Zytec initially got interested—in an industry not known for quality, the company that can make itself the quality supplier can attract new customers. It worked for Zytec; it worked for Wallace. The company's share of the market went from 10 percent in 1987 to 18 percent in 1990.

The Wallace Company, with fewer than three hundred employees, started with quality circles, which are intended to let workers suggest better ways to do what gets done. At Wallace, quality circles didn't work; everyone blamed everyone else for a lack of quality. Instead of everyone cooperating to solve problems, people still competed to be sure someone else got the blame. To be fair, it was a self-directed quality effort that helped to make everyone in the company *aware* of the need for quality, but didn't do much to *achieve* quality. In 1987, realizing that they were making progress, but not nearly quickly enough, the company hired Sanders & Sanders Associates, a Houston quality consulting firm, after executives attended a seminar given by Judith Sanders. In the spring of 1989, the company learned about the Baldrige criteria and adopted those as a standard. The Wallace company tried continual improvement, education and training, participatory management, and teamwork—all the areas that quality experts tend to stress. There were some impressive successes. A quality program in workplace safety was so successful, an insurance company gave Wallace a better rating and reduced its insurance premium by $500,000 annually.

But nothing could match the thrill of the Malcolm Baldrige National Quality Award.

At the award ceremony in Washington in December 1990, consultant Sanders said, "It was like winning the Super Bowl." Commerce Secretary Robert A. Mosbacher, himself a Houston oilman, was described as "looking on with a big smile." President George Bush, a transplanted Texan, handed the small-business award to officers of the Wallace Company. The joy didn't last long. Ten months later, *Business Week* was reporting that unless Wallace could solve its financial problems, the quality company might not survive the month. The year Wallace won, it had sales of $88 million, but it lost $691,000. The company was handling up to eighty requests a day for information on the Baldrige Award, and company officials were flying around the country to talk about it. "We were so busy doing the presentations," John Wallace said, "that we weren't following up and getting the sales." The company had a quality award, but did not make use of the Baldrige Award's business potential, as Zytec had.

The Wallace Company board of directors brought in Cooper in July 1992 to turn the company around. He canceled fifty scheduled speeches by company personnel and fired several executives who had spent more time on the road talking about quality than in Houston producing it. He also fired 25 percent of the staff, the people whose work had won the Baldrige Award. When you're losing $300,000 a month, some expense has to go. Cooper said that between 1988 and 1990, operating expenses had gone up $2 million, largely for employee training. Wallace admitted, "I probably should have moved faster to reduce expenses."

Forbes magazine quoted Cooper as advising, "When you win an award, set it up in the lobby and go back to work." It is excellent advice, and it fits perfectly with the idea of continual improvement—since the race never ends, winning an award is only a pleasant recognition of what you've accomplished in the past. It does not change what remains to be accomplished in the future, nor does the award guarantee that you will be able to accomplish it.

However excellent the advice may be, setting the award in the lobby and going back to work would not have solved what went wrong at Wallace. It might have delayed the crisis, but it would not have prevented it. Cooper's advice recognized an internal problem. Dr. Curt W. Reimann, the director of the Baldrige program, saw an external problem: "A quality program can't protect a company" he said, "from national business trends like the credit crunch and the recession." That's true, but it doesn't explain why Wallace went under and Zytec increased its profits during the same recession.

The difference between Zytec's continuing success and Wallace's bankruptcy was not national business trends or what happened after the Baldrige Award. The critical difference between the two companies is what happened *before* the Baldrige Award.

Schmidt at Zytec considers the Baldrige criteria a "wayside stop" along the route mapped out by the Deming quality philosophy. Compare that to what happened at Wallace. After attending a Baldrige quality conference in April 1989, Michael E. Spiess, a vice president at Wallace, said, "We found that the Baldrige criteria were a good road map to where we wanted to go." John Wallace said, "We were so impressed that we decided that we would redesign our quality program around the criteria in the Baldrige application. . . . The criteria define a TQM philosophy." Wallace believed that the Baldrige represented a total quality management philosophy and also believed that the award criteria were a guide to the future.

At the moment Wallace and his associates made that decision—the decision that measurement is philosophy—they were in trouble. Because company officers did not understand Deming's philosophy and his insistence on "constancy of purpose," they lost track of what they were supposed to do next. What happened at the Wallace Company was exactly what Deming warns against—a company's belief that the Baldrige criteria *define* quality instead of *measuring* it. The Wallace Company's obituary should have said that it died not from a quality program but from the lack of a quality philosophy to guide that program. They looked at a tape measure and saw a carpenter.

6

. . . . .

Deming and Baldrige

More appealing than knowledge itself
is the feeling of knowing.
—*Daniel J. Boorstin*

A continuing complaint that American women have against men is that a man driving a car, no matter how hopelessly lost, would rather be lost than stop and ask directions. That is not always true, but it is true often enough to be a frequent and recognizable theme of cartoons. There are all sorts of explanations, but the most charitable one (and the least likely to be true) says that it expresses some sort of genetic memory of the early explorers who pushed off from Europe without maps, without assistance, and without any guarantee of success or survival to find places that Europeans wanted found. Christopher Columbus "found" the Americas in the late fifteenth century that way. Of course, he was looking for India, but there was no place on the way to stop and ask directions, and he probably wouldn't have anyway.

Each new "finding" contributed to people's knowledge of the world and added detail to the world's maps, which five hundred years ago were rudimentary at best. The concept of locating your place on the globe by longitude and latitude was first suggested by two Greek mathematicians in the third century B.C., but as we mentioned in chapter 2, having the knowledge of what needs to be done and having the know-how to do it are not the same.

What made mapmaking so difficult in the days of Columbus, Vasco da Gama, John Cabot, Ferdinand Magellan, and others was that no one had yet figured out how to accurately measure longitude; that is, the distance a mariner was east or west of the prime meridian, the imaginary line that runs from pole to pole through Greenwich, England. (The international date line is directly opposite, halfway around the earth in the Pacific Ocean, and touches no land mass, although it takes sizable jogs to avoid Siberia, the Aleutian Islands, and some of the South Pacific islands.) Latitude—the distance north or south of the equator—was fairly simple and could be found by measuring the angle from the horizon to the sun. To measure longitude, however, you need to know what time it is, a fact not even suggested until forty years after Columbus sailed from Spain, and it would not have mattered had he known. In the days of Columbus and for a hundred years or more afterward, there was no timepiece that was sufficiently reliable at sea.*

Strictly speaking, a map is not necessary for any voyage, no matter how treacherous, if you are both daring and lucky, but the better the map you have, the less blind luck you will need and the more chance there is that you will succeed. In 1991, Jack Hillerich, president of the Hillerich and Bradsby Company of Louisville, said,

♦ ♦ ♦ ♦ ♦ ♦ ♦ ♦ ♦ ♦

* For those interested, Daniel J. Boorstin's book *The Discoverers* opens with a fascinating and detailed history of how people solved the problem of map making.

"Deming is like the North Star; he is a guide pointing the way."

Consider the management system of Dr. W. Edwards Deming as a complete map of your continual improvement journey toward quality. You will never get there, of course—*continual* means just that—but on the journey, you will be momentarily lost only occasionally, if at all, and you will never run off the map. It will be good forever. The Malcolm Baldrige National Quality Award, on the other hand, provides a highly detailed map of the place where you are *at the moment*, but it can't guide you one step further. The edge of the Baldrige map ought to carry the medieval mapmaker's warning of uncharted territory, "Here be demons."

Baldrige director Reimann has warned, "Competing for the Baldrige Award should be undertaken, I think, with great care by a company. I think it should be a culmination of its commitment to quality. The criteria could be misused by seeing them as a shorthand checklist, not realizing the tremendous thought that has to be put behind every element and the long investment that the leadership of the company has to make." Reimann's statement is not in the Baldrige criteria. Perhaps if his warning were printed on the cover of the criteria booklet (something like the surgeon general's cautions on cigarettes and alcohol), the Wallace Company might not have gone astray.

Even if the warnings were there in bold letters, the written criteria have other shortcomings: They use the word "aim," but not in the sense of what business a company is in, or why it is in that business; the word "system" is also used, but more as a synonym for "process;" and the idea of a management system or a system of thought is not included. The criteria also ignore synthesis, or putting things together in the expanded system, which Dr. Russell Ackoff says "is the key to systems thinking, just as analysis, or taking them apart, was the key to Machine-Age thinking." Philip B. Crosby, consultant and author of *Quality Is Free* and other books, gives six reasons for his opposition to the Baldrige Award, one of which is "Executives are happily passing the criteria package to committees and backing away from the process." The criteria do say leadership's commitment is essential, but they do not explain that what is required is that top management must formally identify the organization's mission, vision, and guiding principles: What are we doing? Why are we doing it?

Despite our misgivings, the Malcolm Baldrige National Quality Award has done more to make Americans aware of quality than any other single thing we know. "Increasingly," Reimann says, "we hear stories about the Baldrige Award that companies plan to apply perhaps five years from now. . . . We also see companies applying for the Baldrige Award in order to get feedback from our Board of Examiners." Reimann says the Baldrige Criteria are sent to perhaps as many as a thousand companies for every company that finally applies. Although we argue with some of the award's details and requirements, we are delighted that the Baldrige Award exists. Our interest is not in getting rid of the award but in making it better. The creation of the award in 1987 by the U.S. Congress may have been that body's most effective contribution so far to America's need for improved quality and productivity.

However, we were unable to persuade Deming of the award's value. He remained opposed to any system not based on his own Profound Knowledge, and he had little faith in government involvement. Despite the success of Zytec, he questioned the use of his 14 Points with the seven Baldrige criteria because, he said, the criteria often send the wrong message and sometimes ask for impossible measurements. (Reimann argues that they are difficult but not impossible.) Nonetheless, some others who have studied Deming's work and are known to be his admirers and students share our view of the Baldrige Award. It is not perfect, but America is better with it than without it. Dr. Myron Tribus says, "The creation of the Baldrige prize has been extraordinarily important. I find people that a few years ago were not interested and were difficult to reach have changed their tune." Dr. Brian Joiner, who heads his own consulting company in Wisconsin, adds, "I think it's really helped to develop a national focus . . . on quality." Joiner was a judge for the award until 1991 and believes the criteria are an excellent way for a company to look at its own quality system and measure whether it is, in fact, achieving the expected results.

The greatest single problem with the Baldrige criteria is that there is no core philosophy, no guiding theory against which to test ideas. "Nothing worthwhile," Tribus says, "is ever done without a sense of passion and commitment. That requires a philosophy. You can't be passionate about guidelines; you can only be compulsive." Reimann argues that you can be compulsive in carrying out the 14 Points. But what Tribus, Deming, and others see as the biggest problem—the lack of a core philosophy—Reimann sees as a plus. He says he would not endorse a specific quality system "even if I were free to do so. . . . The guidelines are nonprescriptive," he says, "in the sense that they do not require a company to implement a particular set of rules or systems because the observations are

that there are many paths to carry out the same aims.
. . . There is no evidence to suggest that one system fits
all."

Since 1987, when Reimann wrote the criteria in next
to no time, they have changed at least slightly every year, a
built-in example of continual improvement. Considering
his lack of time and the possibilities for error, writing criteria that were immediately accepted by American industrial leaders remains a remarkable achievement, and an
achievement that might otherwise not have been possible
at all. If the pace at which he was required to work had
been more leisurely, the backbiting endemic to the quality
field might have destroyed the Baldrige Award before it
was established. It is regrettable, but true, that among the
experts there is a lack of agreement on how to define or
achieve quality. There is also a lack of anything that might
even pass for camaraderie.

"Curt was faced with a very serious problem," Tribus
says. "He had to create an award, but he could not identify
with any of the gurus. . . . If he built a prize that favored the teachings and philosophy of one or another of
these people, he'd be in difficulty." Which meant the
award criteria had to reflect all of the experts, but endorse
none of them. Reimann says the criteria also had to recognize that, as far as he was concerned, "the gurus did not
have all the answers." His search included other quality
examples and methods. "All the enduring truths about
quality," he wrote in 1990, "whether they be Deming's 14
points or someone else's definitions, are all accommo-
dated in this total quality management concept. We believe these seven categories comprehensively define total
quality management."

The 1993 Baldrige Award criteria were in seven categories, twenty-seven subcategories, and ninety-two "areas to address"—that is, specific points that the examiners would want to investigate (appendix C). The criteria booklet each year also includes highly detailed notes to help companies understand exactly what will be expected. A perfect score would be 1,000, which no one has ever received, and in all likelihood, no one ever will. The seven categories are not of equal value. In 1993, customer focus was worth 300 points, but strategic planning was worth only 60. That is explained by the first sentence in the award's "Core Values and Concepts" section: "Quality is judged by the customer."

The points are given because a mathematical score is necessary to explain why it was awarded to one company and not another. "It was necessary," Tribus says, "to come forward with a prize that had objectivity in it in the sense that you could really justify to somebody why company A got it and company B did not." Without a point score, how could anyone explain to an angry member of Congress why some heavy political contributor did not win? Deming would not accept that Baldrige numbers meant anything. "[The criteria] expect everything to be measured. The most important losses and gains," he said, "cannot be measured. It's only the trivial things that can be measured, and that's what the award criteria deal with—what's trivial."

Despite Deming's refusal to endorse the Baldrige Award and Reimann's refusal to adopt the Deming philosophy, the experience at Zytec demonstrates that the Deming management system can be used to win the Baldrige Award. We have determined which of Deming's 14 Points apply to each of the Baldrige criteria. Our conclusions are based on work done earlier by William

Scherkenbach, a quality consultant, author, and former student of Deming's, and we've checked with him to be sure we weren't inadvertently leading you astray.* (Keep in mind that we are reporters, not statisticians.)

We also don't want to lead you astray on what you can do with this information. You can *not* set out to win the Malcolm Baldrige National Quality Award by using Deming's 14 Points. You *can* use the complete Deming management system to improve quality in your company and then, if you want, you can apply for the award and use the 14 Points to help satisfy the seven Baldrige criteria. Figure 2 provides a handy reference. If you try to win the Baldrige prize without a quality management system in place, you may well run off the edge of the map and fall into the land of the demons, and they are vicious and unforgiving.

◆　◆　◆

Category One:
Leadership

"Leadership," Reimann says, "is the first category because of our belief that the entire quality system will flow from the attention and commitment of the leaders of the corporation or, indeed, any organization." The importance of the senior executive in achieving quality is one of the few things on which all quality experts agree. Deming's often-

◆　◆　◆　◆　◆　◆　◆　◆　◆　◆

* The work was done by Beth Bernstein, who studied the 14 Points and the Baldrige categories, decided what went where, then talked with Scherkenbach and Deming to get agreement on meanings. That was a good deal more difficult than it sounds.

Figure 2

BALDRIGE CATEGORIES

14 POINTS	I Leadership	II Information and Analysis	III Strategic Quality Planning	IV Human Resource Development and Management	V Management of Process Quality	VI Quality and Operational Results	VII Customer Focus and Satisfaction
1. Constancy	•		•				
2. New Philosophy	•		•		•		•
3. Cease Inspection		•	•		•		
4. Partner Suppliers			•		•	•	
5. Improve Constantly	•	•	•	•	•	•	•
6. Institute Training				•	•		•
7. Institute Leadership	•	•		•			
8. Drive out fear	•			•			
9. Eliminate Barriers	•	•	•	•	•	•	
10. Eliminate Slogans	•			•			
11. No Quotas		•	•	•			
12. Increase Joy	•			•			•
13. Institute Education			•	•	•		•
14. Do it	•		•			•	•

cited comment was "Quality is made in the boardroom," and he was adamant that the chief executive, and only the chief executive, is responsible for quality, and he cannot delegate that responsibility.

The leadership category is broken down into three subcategories, each of which has four areas to address. One of those is the "senior executives' leadership, personal involvement, and visibility" in the quality effort. Deming's reaction was one of scorn. "He could work his head off," he said, "doing the wrong thing. Where's any word whatever in the guidelines about his understanding of a system? Not a word." The guidelines question how senior executives "evaluate and improve" their effectiveness, which set Deming off again. "As if you could evaluate such things," he thundered. "Wrong! Wrong teaching!"

Brian Joiner says the category is nothing more than a series of questions that can be answered: "Are its leaders really focusing on quality? Are they really understanding quality? Are they really managing in that kind of way? Are they really getting the best from their people? Are they really working with their people well? Are they really finding out what barriers people have to being able to do a good job?" Seen from that perspective, nine of Deming's 14 Points are useful in Category One.

You cannot lead an organization toward quality without constancy of purpose (point 1), and it is the job of senior management not only to adopt the new philosophy of cooperation but to teach it to employees, customers, and suppliers (point 2). John O. Grettenberger, vice president of GM and general manager of its Cadillac division, a Baldrige winner in 1990, said of his company's success with Deming, "We knew that we had to turn the company around, and we knew that we couldn't ask others to change until we, the leaders of the organization, demonstrated a willingness to do so ourselves." The leader also has to set the example of continual improvement (point 5).* The senior executive has the responsibility to institute leadership (point 7), drive out fear (point 8), eliminate barriers to cooperation (point 9), eliminate slogans (point 10), create an atmosphere in which people can take joy in their work by getting rid of personal ratings and ranking (point 12), and, of course, no one but the senior executives can lead in the transformation from a quantity to a quality method (point 14).

◆　◆　◆

Category Two:
Information and Analysis

The category has three subcategories and eleven areas to address. Essentially, the question is how much information have you collected to help drive the company toward quality, and how did you collect it? Included in this category are goals and "benchmarking," the popular management practice of going to look at the best in the world at any specific function to see how that company does it. Benchmarking has three immediate benefits that sometimes get overlooked. First, as Reimann points out, it helps foster a spirit of sharing. Second, benchmarking

◆　◆　◆　◆　◆　◆　◆　◆　◆　◆

* Continual improvement shows up in each of the seven Baldrige categories, the only one of the 14 Points that does.

can help Americans get past the ugly, chauvinistic not-invented-here habit, which automatically and childishly dismisses anything an American did not think of first. Third, it ends the necessity of reinventing the wheel in every company. Once a better way to do anything is in place, anyone else can adopt and continually improve it—with a couple of monumental provisos. We'll get to those, but let's start with goals.

Deming did not like goals because they focus on the result and not *how* the result was achieved. In a conversation the two men had, Reimann told Deming, "If your competitor is putting a product out with one-tenth the defects that your product has, you need to know something about that, and you need to organize your work force to achieve this goal of improvement." Deming didn't accept that. "A goal doesn't help anybody," he said. "By what method are the only three words that count. By what method?" His point is that focusing on the goal rather than the method of achieving quality could lead senior executives to rate people or departments on whether goals were achieved, thereby establishing ultimately destructive competitions and changing the focus from management changes to worker goals.

Benchmarking can also lead to result-oriented goals and to ill-informed copying. "There's danger," Joiner says, "that companies just go and copy one another without understanding. That, of course, won't work. . . . I think they still need to understand a theory of how to achieve that." Unless you know *why* something works, knowing that it works in a particular circumstance is of limited value. "An example teaches nothing," Deming said, "unless studied with the aid of theory; otherwise people merely copy. They get into trouble . . . because they did not understand *why* something was good or *why* something was bad."

Reimann does not argue against the necessity of theory, but he does argue that "we cannot give awards based on philosophy." Why, he asks, does theory have to come first? "The first stages of benchmarking or comparison may very well be merely looking for and at things that can be copied. But I believe that the successful companies take it back, and there is a great deal of theory and discussion, so I don't believe theory need precede benchmarking. I think that benchmarking can drive interest in theory. In effect," he says, "companies wake up to wholly new ways of doing things."

That is possible, but it is not guaranteed, as it would be if a theory were already in place. A theory would also prevent a second problem—distraction. Scherkenbach says the quality company must always be focused on the customer but use peripheral vision to be aware of the competitor. "You need to learn from your competitors," he says; "you need to learn from everybody, but that should not take your focus off the customer." Deming said that all the time and effort we have put into studying the competition would have been better spent studying the customers and what could be done for them. In other words, collecting information is important, but what kind of information you collect, how and from whom you collect it, and what use you make of it are even more important. Information from the customer must be fed back into your system; information from the competitor may or may not be. That is difficult for some people to understand. They insist that the competitor must be watched.

True, it would be foolish to ignore the competitor, but it would be even more foolish to ignore the customer. The competitor cannot put you out of business. The competitor can do only what you do—offer products and services for sale. The customer picks one or the other of the products to buy, and the customer's choice determines who will stay in business and who will be forced out. To stay in business, you must learn what your customer's needs are and produce innovative products to meet and exceed them. The idea is to stay ahead of the customer's expectations. If you have been feeding information from the customer back into your system to continually improve and delight that customer and stay ahead of his needs, why would he buy from your competitor?

To score points with the Baldrige examiners, you can cease mass inspection (point 3) because you are going to continually improve (point 5) the system using data. Leaders need education (point 13) to know what data are important and how to analyze them. Leaders have to know the difference between common and special causes of variation, and everyone needs training (point 6) to be able to contribute to improvements. None of this can happen without leadership (point 7) to break down barriers to cooperation (point 9) and get rid of quotas (point 11).

To put it another way, you are applying elements of Profound Knowledge to test ideas for improvement gained through benchmarking (or anything else) and to test information from customers. You must always keep firmly in mind *why* you are gathering information and *what* use you will make of it, and you must realize that if you do not have a theory against which to test that information, then that information will do limited good at best and might do incredible harm. We have found too many people who think information-tested-by-theory is something they can more or less be vaguely aware of, then ignore. It doesn't work that way. If you screw this one up, you are screwed for fair, and that's it.

◆ ◆ ◆

Category Three:
Strategic Quality Planning

Category Three has two subcategories and eight areas to address. Essentially, the Baldrige examiners want to know the company's processes for planning, short- and long-term goals, how those goals are integrated into business planning, and how those goals will improve quality throughout the company. The use of the word "goals" creates immediate problems since the Deming method insists that the goal itself is unimportant; what is important is how you plan to achieve it. Therefore, think of the Baldrige word "goal" more in the sense of Deming's concept of "aim" than in the sense of "target." You are not trying to do some specific thing by Thursday; you are trying to ensure long-term success. "The job of management," Deming said, "is to fix the aim, state the aim . . . not what we're doing, but what we ought to be doing, and to understand how to do it." It is somewhat easier to understand as Joiner explains it. "Planning goals," he says, "should not be used until the organization understands that the goals will be used to plan, not to judge outcomes." In a traditional organization, if a goal-target isn't reached, someone must have done something wrong, so a scapegoat must be found and made to pay. In a quality organization, the long-term goal-aim of the organization is what drives the system in a cooperative effort for continual improvement.

You know right away that constancy of purpose (point 1) and adopting the new philosophy (point 2) are critical in this category.* When top leaders take the responsibility for strategic planning for long-term gains, then short-term inspections can be eliminated (point 3), and to get improvements and reach those goal-aims, the organization will have to make partners of its suppliers (point 4), and everyone in the system, including suppliers, will have to work on improvement (point 5). You can't plan on long-term improvement without training and education (points 6 and 13). You have to make it possible for everyone to work together to achieve the goal-aim (point 9), and people must understand the difference between the goal-aim and a quota, which you don't need (point 11). If you don't all get together and get the job done (point 14), then the whole exercise is fruitless anyway.

Strategic planning is critical. "The leaders," Scherkenbach writes, "have to *plan* ways to test new ideas, processes and products in order to reach those improvement goals. And the strategic plans have to include methods for encouraging innovation." In an article describing the quality approach in the Department of the Navy, three people who were involved write that the strategic plan "describes the mission, vision, guiding principles, strategic goals, and strategies an organization intends to pursue over a ten-to-twenty-year period. It serves as a

* * * * * * * * * *

* Ten of the 14 Points apply to Category Three, more than to any other category.

clear and enduring statement of an organization's intention for its employees, customers, and suppliers."

This is a good place to bring up another Deming technique, called the Shewhart Cycle, named for Walter Shewhart, a pioneer in statistical analysis of quality, who designed it. Almost always it will be abbreviated PDCA, but Deming changed it a couple of years ago to PDSA, which stands for Plan-Do-Study-Act. (The old C stood for "Check," and Deming decided that was the wrong word.) The Shewhart Cycle (figure 3) helps ensure continual improvement, and it's simple enough to explain; obviously, it's more difficult to do.

THE SHEWHART CYCLE

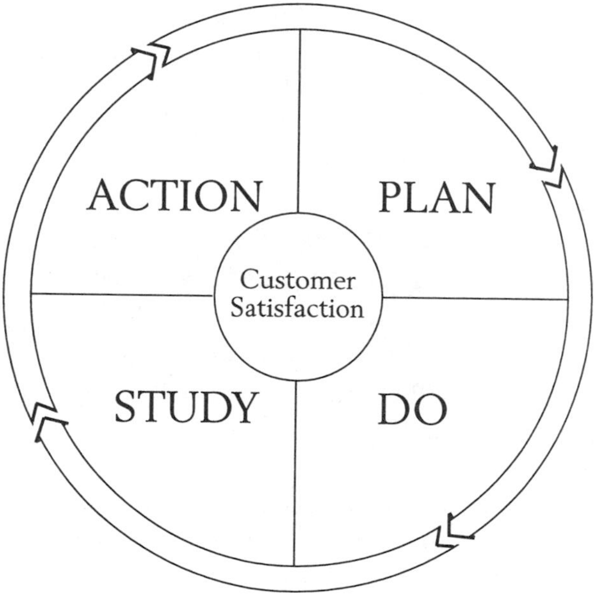

ACTION   PLAN

Customer
Satisfaction

STUDY   DO

Figure 3

You *Plan* a change, an improvement, something you think will work. Planning is where you spend your time. If the experiment isn't planned correctly, you may not find out what you want to know. As much as half of the time available goes into planning.

You experiment; that is, you *Do* what you planned, and you do it on the smallest scale possible to limit the damage in case you're wrong. If you are pushing for the greatest possible improvement in the shortest possible time, sometimes you will definitely be wrong. You'll only be harmed if you've made this a universal test.

Study the results. Did you get what you'd hope you'd get? What did the test demonstrate? Be careful not to read into the results what you wanted or hoped to find.

Finally, you *Act* on your study. You either put the improvement into effect, modify it and start the cycle all over with another plan, or throw the whole thing out, march back to square one, and start again.

◆ ◆ ◆

Category Four:
Human Resource Development and Management

Human Resources has five subcategories and eighteen areas to address. Only the seventh category, Customer Focus and Satisfaction, asks for more specific details. Human resource development is concerned with how you make it possible for your people to grow and develop so that they can do all they are capable of doing to achieve the company's objectives. Among the specifics the examiners look for are the rates of employee turnover, absenteeism, and safety records—three excellent indicators of morale.

Deming was critical of the category for two reasons.

First, employee morale could be high, absenteeism and employee turnover low, and training and education programs excellent, and the organization might still go out of business either because the organization was working toward the wrong aim or because it was building a product—a buggy whip, for example—that no one wanted. By focusing on employees in this category, Deming believes attention is drawn away from management at the top. "The work force," he said every chance he got, "is *not* the problem!" He recited some of the Baldrige criteria areas to address, then dismissed them. "Emphasis is wrong," he insisted. "The work force is what you don't have to worry about. Quality is made at the top, in the boardroom." What is required for success is a quality management system and knowledge of how it works among the most senior executives.

Reimann argues that many of Deming's objections are obvious and could only be a problem if this category stood alone. It does not, he says; it is tied to the other categories and to the key result indicators. However, the criteria do not say clearly that to have a successful quality system the company must first have defined a mission, vision, and guiding principles. Thousands of companies get the criteria and except for the one in one thousand that applies, there is no way to know what use is being made of the material. What is obvious to Reimann may or may not be obvious to others.

Reimann defends the category for what it is achieving in those companies that do apply. "In many corporations," he says, "there have not been very high investments in training or education for employees, and this award has certainly promoted [training and education]." He says all the award winners invest heavily in training and education, well above the national average. "Several of the companies [winners]," he says, "are the outstanding national leaders."

There is a national need for more education and training. American business and industry already spend about $30 billion annually on training and education, but only a handful of the largest corporations spend any money at all, and most of the money spent is used to educate and train managers, not employees. Just as the Malcolm Baldrige National Quality Award is designed to make people aware of quality, Category Four is designed to make senior executives aware of the payoff of investments in training and education.

Dr. Herbert E. Striner, former dean of Kogod Business School at American University, has argued for years that those countries that make the biggest investments in their people tend to have the most successful economies. Deming seemed to agree with that. "Obviously," he said, "if there are no [education and training] programs, there's no hope for growth. The problem is managers basing their actions on meaningless measurements." Dr. Gipsie Ranney, a quality consultant, tells managers at General Motors, "You can't look at the performance of any individual independent of the effect of the other individuals that he or she has to work with and the system within which they all work. You can't separate out the individual's performance." Again, it is the lesson of the Red Bead Experiment: The individual's performance is a result of the system; the individual cannot make it better, and only through acts of willful rebellion can he even make it worse.

The second of Deming's complaints is that Category Four asks for measurements that are not possible, such as the effectiveness of employee training and education. Robert Galvin, who as CEO at Motorola introduced the Six Sigma management system there, said that in the beginning a quality system required a "leap of faith" that it would never cost the company money, that in the long run, every dime spent on training and education would come back and then some. Deming agreed. "Training for skills," he said, "is one of those examples in which one is guided by theory, not by figures. One may spend, say, twenty thousand dollars for training a group of people, for improving their skills, but one will never be able to measure the benefit of it. The cost we know . . . the benefit we shall never know." The money is spent, as Galvin said, on a "leap of faith." Deming said the money must be spent, "because we believe that it will pay off, that it will help our people, give them a chance for joy in work, and that we'll get our money back and a lot more." That is belief, not certainty, and if there is anecdotal evidence that it is true—as we believe it is—there remains no way to measure it. To demonstrate the point to yourself, try to answer the question "How much money must be spent on training to guarantee a 10 percent increase in work force performance?"

Among those who are ardent advocates of statistical process control, that unanswerable question can create a problem. A popular saying among them is "You can't manage what you can't measure." Deming's approach is exactly the opposite. "The job of managers," he said, "is to manage what can't be measured." There is no way to measure what most people do most of the time, yet no organization can survive if people are not managed. As we mentioned before, there is no way to measure whether you are getting high-value, discretionary work from the employees, but the theory of a quality management system says that you will get it if your management system makes it possible and pleasant for the employee to give it. Can that be proved? It appears to be true and logically should be true, but it cannot be proved. It is, as Deming so often argued, the importance of theory over numbers. "The most important losses and gains," he said, "cannot be measured, but they're the ones we must manage."

To prevent some confusion (and maybe cause some as well), a manager deals with areas that can be measured and areas that cannot be measured. Areas that can be measured should be measured to provide data on which to make decisions. In those areas that cannot be measured, a manager can and should make value judgments. Is this training course worthwhile? A good manager can answer that question without taking measurements.

Here's where it gets more complicated. You *can* measure some training. It's no trick to measure whether a typing course helped typists improve their speed; a count of the words-per-minute typed at the beginning of the class and at the end will show you the improvement. But what count do you take to measure the effectiveness of a class in how to be a team leader or how to build consensus?

Now to really make your life miserable, let's take one more step. From a *theoretical*, scientific point of view, it is possible to measure anything. However, the way to take the measurement is so complex and inadequate that from a *practical* point of view, some things cannot be measured. "There is beginning to be," Reimann says, "a discipline centered around measurement. We're not far from having more to draw on here."

Another problem area for Deming was tying short-term reward and recognition systems to individual performance, which Category Four covers. Reimann says the Baldrige Award does not require employee rankings. "I don't agree," he says, "that we're seeing in these guidelines a prescription that, for example, companies must have a performance appraisal system, or they must rank employees. We've seen it both ways, and we've seen success both ways." Examiners say that what they judge is what the company does, and if the company follows the Deming management system and does not rank employees, that's fine. A careful reading of the areas to address does indicate there is less concern with pure numbers than there is with indications that organizations realize the importance of their people and are doing what they can to improve their people and the environment in which they work.

Reimann thinks the Baldrige Award may be changing the way companies think. "We're seeing many experiments being performed," he says, "including some involving the abolishment of ranking systems. In other cases, we have not seen those abolished. So we feel that we're providing a kind of national experiment . . . in visibility and sharing of experiences."

To use the Deming management system within the Baldrige criteria in Category Four, you know you are going to start with points 6 and 13, training and education.

Now we make a sharp turn and speed down a four-lane tangent.

Until the summer of 1993, Deming insisted that education was best if it had nothing to do with the job at hand. He wanted education to expand horizons; he did not want it focused on the minutiae of accounting or computer programming or marketing. At a seminar in Texas in 1988, he was upset with the Ford Motor Company because it would not let employees study basketball as education. (Ford has arranged with the United Auto Workers to have free education programs for Ford employees at every facility.) Deming's point was that basketball taught teamwork even better than if you set up a skills course called "Teamwork." He believed people should learn teamwork not just on the job, but in life as well. "Pretty important," he said, "pretty important!" He insisted on a strict separation between skills training (point 6), designed to give you those abilities you need to improve your work, and education (point 13), designed to give you those abilities you need in order to grow as a person and better *understand* yourself and your work and the world around you.

While the research for this chapter was going on, Deming reconsidered his strict separation of the two and wondered if it was *too* strict a separation. For instance, could not the teaching of Profound Knowledge and the 14 Points come under education? They are not, in a strict sense, job skills, but there is no doubt that a worker would be better off knowing them and applying them not only at work, but at home as well. Is that education or training? Deming had not decided at the time he died. We suggest that you think of training and education this way: If it is a lesson on how to use a screwdriver, it is training; if it is a lesson on Plato's *Republic*, it is education. Otherwise, if it applies mainly to the job, it's likely to be training, and if it applies mainly to everything else and to the job only by extension, it is likely to be education. Anything else is certainly one or the other, or maybe both.

Thank God we got that cleared up!

Under either the strict or the not-so-strict interpretation of point 13, education would apply to Category Four, Human Resource Development, as would point 6, skills training. Since the workers cannot establish education and training programs on their own, the organization will need leadership (point 7) to get the programs started and continual improvement (point 5) to better respond to the employees' needs. This will make the employees better able to contribute to the organization's success, and people will find joy in their work (point 12) when they can make a contribution. To do that, leaders will have to eliminate barriers to cooperation (point 9), cease those practices like employee rankings that cause fear (point 8), and get rid of slogans (point 10) and quotas (point 11).

The object of human resource development is to establish trust, to demonstrate that the company believes in the importance and worth of the employees. "Without trust," Grettenberger of Cadillac says, "it is impossible to get people to participate." Without the active participation and cooperation of everyone involved, the organization can never achieve what it could *with* participation and cooperation. What you are trying to develop are knowledge and know-how, and both of those can be learned.

• • •

Category Five:
Management of Process Quality

This category includes five subcategories and fifteen areas to address, all of which involve "systematic processes the company used to pursue ever-higher quality and company operational performance." The category includes research and development, design, how you work with suppliers to improve what they do, how you keep up with and improve what's being produced, and how you track down and eliminate common problems. The points in the category are so universally accepted that there is no argument.

You would cease inspection (point 3) because inspection cannot improve your quality, but adopting a win-win philosophy (point 2) can. As the category specifically includes suppliers, then what you are doing to make your suppliers partners (point 4) is going to be critical. Training and education (points 6 and 13) will be important, as will eliminating the barriers to cooperation (point 9). All of you and all of your processes must continually improve (point 5).

♦ ♦ ♦

Category Six:
Quality and Operational Results

With four subcategories and eight areas to address, this category is about company quality, supplier quality, and "improvement trends." Applicants have to compare their own quality levels to those of competitors and benchmark companies. The category requires a good deal of measurement.

The danger in Category Six and in the data analysis section of Category Two is that without an understanding of systems and variation, there is no way of knowing where the results are coming from or what all that information means. Do the variations in results reflect common causes or special causes? (This question also comes up in Category Five.) To put it in other words, is the system itself messed up internally, or did the assembly line just get hit by lightning? If you don't know the answer, you cannot improve what's coming off the line. You also have to look for variation in patterns and trends in results over a period of time to be sure that what you're doing is working. "If we want better results," Deming told a group, "we have to improve our method. Any attempt to beat the system will impair the outcome of some other part of the company." The object, you remember, is to make the company as a whole (the system) work as best it can. Improving only one part of it (one process) only causes problems in other parts.

Since this category deals with results, remember that the Shewhart Cycle explained in Category Three can be helpful—Plan-Do-Study-Act.

The points necessary in Category Six are—surprise!—continual improvement (point 5), working with your suppliers (point 4), breaking down barriers to cooperation (point 9), and transforming the organization from a quantity to a quality company (point 14).

• • •

Category Seven:
Customer Focus and Satisfaction

This one counts for nearly a third of an applicant's score, and it is the largest of the seven, with six subcategories and twenty areas to address. The examiners want to know the nature of a company's relationship with its customers, and how the company knows what that relationship is;

that is, how did the company get its information? The examiners also want to know what the company believes the customer's expectations are now and in the future. Is the customer satisfied, and how does the company know? What are the methods of improving customer satisfaction, and how do results compare with the competition?

Trying to satisfy this category forces a company to think systematically about its customers and how to get accurate information about their needs and desires and their satisfaction or lack of it. "They have done that informally," Joiner says, "but they may not have a documented system to do that." As with Category Five, there is little or no disagreement among the experts about how critical it is stay ahead of your customers. The point of the Baldrige Award criteria is that you cannot stay ahead of them unless you have a system in place to find out what they want.

It doesn't stop there. Part of what you must do with the customer is, in Deming's words, "teach him about needs that he does not yet know he has." If you don't tell him, the customer cannot know how much you can do for him; conversely, if you don't learn from the customer what he thinks he needs, you can't improve your system to meet or exceed those needs. The customer must be part of your expanded system as well as the focus of what you do. Grettenberger says, "You know, every individual in the organization needs to have the opportunity to add value to the customer." Frederick W. Smith, who founded Federal Express, the first service industry winner of the Baldrige, said in 1990, "We have grown to realize that customer satisfaction must begin with employee satisfaction. All the more reason, therefore, to create a workplace that responds to the human desire to be part of a greater mission, one in which everyone can contribute and make a difference." That allows them to get joy from their work (point 12), but they must be educated to the importance of the customer, and the customer must be educated about the ability of the company (point 13). Employees, therefore, will need training (point 6) to work and communicate with customers. None of that is possible until everyone in the company has adopted the new philosophy (point 2), is involved in transforming the company (point 14), and is working cooperatively to continually improve (point 5).

◆　◆　◆　◆　◆

We intend only to illustrate how you might, if you wish, apply Deming's 14 Points to the Baldrige criteria. We do not intend to make the 14 Points separate little things to do. They are not. The 14 Points represent a way to use Profound Knowledge, the four parts of which—systems, variation, knowledge, psychology—are the framework of the Deming philosophy. The 14 Points are designed to let you apply that philosophy in specific situations.

The Baldrige criteria are loaded with good and useful ideas, but they do not embody a systematic approach driven by a philosophy. That leaves organizations with "things to do"—seven categories, twenty-eight subcategories, ninety-two areas to address. Reimann insists that the goals and core values discussed in the criteria are "the essence of a systematic approach." With respect, that may be true if you are a scientist or a quality consultant with a background in statistics, but it was not true for us after several readings of the criteria, and, we suspect, it would not be true for most business people who pick up the criteria booklet and try to understand it.

In truth, there is only one thing any organization needs to do: It needs to change from a quantity to a quality management system, and in order to do that, corporate leaders must first understand that the old quantity system that focused exclusively on results cannot be improved by grafting on good, new ideas. A new culture and system must be created to replace the old one, and the new system must focus on the philosophy of continual improvement. It must start with a formal definition from the company's leaders of the company's mission, vision, and guiding principles.

Once again, we return to our original point: America is better off—perhaps even *much* better off—with the Malcolm Baldrige National Quality Award than it would be without it. The increased public awareness of the need for quality systems alone would make the award worthwhile. "We're hearing more and more," Reimann told Deming, "about the importance of quality principles in schools, in hospitals, in government agencies. I think that these are all very, very positive developments."

So says he; so say we all.

7

• • • • •

Baldrige History

We can do and we've got to do
better than this.*
—*Dr. Seuss*

From 1948 through 1973, income in the United States increased with enough regularity to guarantee that each generation would live better than the one before; that is, children would always live better than their parents had lived. That is no longer true. At the current rate of growth, the improvement that we used to achieve in a single generation will take a full century—about *five* generations. Simply put, our economy does not perform as well as it used to because our productivity has slipped. Productivity is how much is turned out compared with how much is put in. The more you get for less, the higher your productivity is and the better off you are.

There is some disagreement about the figures, but it is generally accepted that productivity increased more than 3 percent a year from 1947 to 1966, then suddenly dropped to just under 2 percent, and by 1973, productivity stopped growing. Between 1973 and 1974, for the first

• • • • • • • • •

* Asked if he had any message he wanted to leave, Theodore Seuss Geisel gave this "slogan" for the United States to a reporter for the *San Diego Union* shortly before his death in September 1991.

time in twenty-five years, productivity dropped by 1.8 percent. No one has ever been able to adequately explain exactly why that happened, but the rate of productivity improvement—our rate of economic growth, if you will—started to fall. As a result, real income—the difference between pay increases and inflation increases—has been shrinking since 1973. Any number of theories have been advanced to explain what happened, and you can get endless argument on what's wrong, what caused it, who's to blame, and how to get out of it. If there is little agreement on anything else, almost everyone will agree that *something* is wrong.

Early in 1993, the news media reported, with some enthusiasm, an increase for 1992 in our national productivity, a quite substantial increase for the first time in years. National business productivity went up 2.8 percent, which doesn't sound like much until you realize that the average increase for the years 1976 to 1991 was less than 1 percent—0.8 to be exact. Later in the year, the Council on Competitiveness, a private business group, said the standard of living had gone up 1.1 percent in the United States in 1992, the first increase in three years. That came from the increase in productivity. If the United States could continue to improve productivity as much as, or even more than, it did in 1992, some of our problems would go away—not all of them, certainly, but some.

However, the productivity increase in 1992 was probably a one-time blip caused by the firing of a huge number of workers. Those who still had jobs took up the slack rather than face unemployment themselves. When a great many people get fired, productivity improves, but only temporarily. We expect to see one more upward blip in the relatively near future when the United States begins to feel the full productivity power of computer technology. Paul David, a professor of economic history at Stanford University, says we have not yet realized that gain, but we're about due. New technology takes several years to make a big difference in productivity.

Unfortunately, two blips don't make a solution. There is a fundamental problem that has not been solved; it hasn't even been recognized as a problem. What led to the drop in productivity growth, we suggest, is the system of traditional American management.

Since 1965, manufacturing productivity, which measures only manufacturing, not services or agriculture, has been going up in Japan at least twice as fast as it has in the United States, even though there has been a falloff in Japan as well. If manufacturing productivity is going up twice as fast in Japan, and technology is about the same in both countries, and capital is available in both, it must mean either that (a) Japanese plant workers work twice as hard as American workers or (b) Japanese plants are run twice as effectively by their management as American plants.

Japanese workers do not work harder. If that were the answer, how could anyone explain the success of the Honda plant in Ohio or the Sony plant in California, to mention only two, where the employees are American? Why do British workers perform better in Japanese-run plants in Great Britain than they do in plants run by British managers? The argument that Japanese workers are somehow more efficient or more cooperative or faster or more subservient or all those other theories that have been advanced over the past fifteen years does not stand up to even casual investigation. Blaming the difference on workers is blatant and transparent evasion by those who won't accept the fact that Japanese plants are more effectively managed. Major Japanese corporations use quality methods of management that were taught to them after World War II by Americans.*

The difference in management techniques became obvious in the United States in the 1960s and '70s when American consumer electronic products were being replaced in an increasingly global market by Japanese products, which were less expensive, better built, and offered more desirable features. After years of saying the Japanese success was caused by cheap labor, societal differences, or international cheating, American companies started to send executives to Japan to study what Japanese management was doing to drive productivity up.

The federal government had started measuring productivity in the 1890s when members of Congress worried about "the displacement of labor by machinery," and it wasn't until World War II that the concern shifted from displacement of workers to improvement of the economy. When productivity started to slip in the 1960s, the government had the figures to show *what* was happening, but like industry, it had nothing to explain *why*. In June 1970, President Richard Nixon proposed a National Commission on Productivity to study the problem, and the Republican Congress approved it.† The commission, among other things, was to make it possible for government, labor, and management to work together to improve American pro-

◆ ◆ ◆ ◆ ◆ ◆ ◆ ◆ ◆ ◆

* For a detailed history, see *Quality or Else*, chapter 1.

† Over the years, it had four different names. Sometimes it was independent, sometimes under other agencies. Its job always remained the same: Find out what was going wrong with productivity.

ductivity. It began to study American management techniques, efficiency and cost in health care, local government, transportation, and the environment, and it helped sponsor a study of Japanese companies.

The commission was established in June 1970 as part of Nixon's Cost of Living Council. In 1972, John Stewart, now a director with McKinsey & Company, arrived to take over as its first nongovernment executive director.

When the commission went to Congress in July 1973 to get its own appropriation for the next year, the problem of productivity was worse than it had been in 1970. Nothing good had happened in three years, and to a member of the House of Representatives, who must stand for reelection every two years, three years is forever. Representative H. R. Gross (R-Iowa) argued against the commission. "Despite the expenditure of $2.5 million on this Commission in the past year," he said, "productivity went down and not up. Will we get a further down-curve in productivity with the expenditure of this $5 million?" Another congressman added his opinion: "I think most of our employees, including the floor sweepers, know more about [productivity] than the Government people."

Representative William Scherle (R-Iowa) saw it as something more sinister; he saw the commission as the start of government industrial policy, interference in the free-market system. He urged his colleagues to vote against the appropriation and "let the United States flow free as a competitive nation. That would be doing everybody a favor." The House voted 239 to 174 not to give the Productivity Commission any more money.

That should have been the end of it, but Washington does not work that way. Through a mutual friend, Executive Director Stewart managed to have dinner with

Scherle. The other two dinner guests were a federal judge and President Nixon's personal attorney. The attorney, the judge, and Stewart made the pitch to fund the commission, to let it continue its work. Scherle was persuaded. Stewart recalls that over dessert, Scherle turned to him and made a bizarre comment: "I will be for or against your commission," Scherle said, "whichever will help you the most."

Being *for* helped the most. Scherle proposed a reconsideration of the appropriation in the House, and this time the Productivity Commission got its money. Government, business, and labor leaders continued to meet and talk about productivity. They agreed it was a long-term problem; they did not agree on what to do to solve it. In 1978, the commission went out of business. A new Democratic administration had no interest in continuing a displaced Republican administration's project. George Kuper, then executive director, recalls a handwritten note from the White House that said, "We don't see anything in this for us." Vice President Walter Mondale declined to succeed Vice President Nelson Rockefeller as chairman. President Jimmy Carter made no appointments to the commission.

Kuper started an orderly shutdown, but had to get a federal court injunction to prevent the General Services Administration from spending money to move the commission to new quarters for the last sixty days. For the Productivity Commission, being born had been easy; living and dying were tough. In the end, Kuper, who had been with the commission since 1972, returned the unspent funds to the federal government and joined the Chamber of Commerce of the United States as a private consultant to plan a national productivity program for that group.

The Productivity Commission lasted from June 1970 to September 1978 and involved government, labor, and business leaders in discussions, but those talks had not led to a solution, or even to a broad recommendation for a long-term effort. Its report in 1975 asked for a "productivity voice" in the development of national policy. It mentioned human resources, capital investment, technology, government regulation, but there was not a hint that managers needed to change the way they managed. The final report three years later was not much different. It concluded that ten areas needed "attention now if we are to reverse the present downward course of the rate of productivity improvement." The ten were all familiar, and nowhere in the ninety-two-page report is there any suggestion that managing for quality is different from managing for quantity.

The Carter White House held a conference on productivity in 1979, but the participants were no more productive than the commission had been. They agreed that the problem was major, but they recommended no action. Some agencies tried their own solutions—the Commerce Department helped small businesses learn about new technology—but there was no governmentwide effort to get American productivity moving up again, nor was there even a public discussion about what to do.

On January 20, 1981, Ronald Reagan was sworn in as the forty-first president of the United States. The slogan of his campaign had been "Get the Government Off Our Backs," and in his inaugural address that day, he said, "Government is not the solution to our problem. Government is the problem." When the Reagan White House originally opposed a suggestion that there be another White House Conference on Productivity, critics assumed that the "government-as-problem" ideology was the reason. The reason was much simpler than that—poor presidential performance.

Myron Tribus, who was assistant secretary for science and technology in the Department of Commerce in the Nixon Administration, remembers that the trouble started with President Reagan's White House Conference on Aging in late 1981. What everyone thought was a wonderful idea turned into a publicity disaster. "The president appeared in the Rose Garden," Tribus says, "with a bunch of [angry] elderly people, and they were all over him on what he was doing *to* the elderly. It was a great embarrassment because he didn't know what to say or how to handle it." Reagan, an actor by training and experience, was wonderful when he had a script, but not nearly so adept when he had to answer off the top of his head. White House Chief of Staff Edwin Meese ruled out any future White House conferences.

Not quite a year later, Representative John J. LaFalce (D-N.Y.) proposed a new conference on productivity; Meese said that the White House would have nothing to do with it. In the wonderful world of official Washington, as we know, a categorical rejection is sometimes only a temporary setback. The proposal to hold a conference on productivity was attached to a bill in the Congress that President Reagan wanted. When he signed the bill he wanted, he thereby approved the productivity conference he didn't want. It all happened within three weeks. But as with rejection, categorical approval isn't all that absolute either. Meese arranged for four regional conferences to be held in June, July, and August 1983 in Durham (North Carolina), St. Louis, San Diego, and Pittsburgh. Surprising, embarrassing, or angry questions could be contained within those regional meetings, where the president would not be. Speakers for the main conference would be auditioning, if you will, during the regional meetings. What they would say at the White House conference would be known in advance. "It was a highly structured affair," Tribus recalls. He testified at the San Diego conference, but was not invited to the White House conference on September 22, 1983. It began with scripted remarks by President Reagan. "The challenge of greater productivity growth," the president said, "is of supreme importance to America's future." *

In the final report from the conference, thirty reasons are given for the decline of American productivity. One of them is "antagonism between the public and private sectors," followed shortly by "government regulations" and "growing reliance on government to solve problems that are social in origin." If those are to be expected from a Republican White House that was long on conservative ideology, another is something of a surprise. Criticism of American management is not high on the Republican agenda, but one of the thirty suspected reasons listed is "outdated management skills and a myopia that emphasizes quantity rather than quality."

In the twentieth century, the United States had been the world's leader in quantity. Mass production was, essentially, an American invention, and without it the standard of living in the United States and around the world would have been much lower. It would have been foolish for a nation as small as Japan, its industrial base destroyed

◆　◆　◆　◆　◆　◆　◆　◆　◆　◆

* Later in the speech, I was quoted by the president, the only time, I think, my name has been mentioned in the White House. (L.D.)

by the war, to have even imagined competing in quantity against the United States. After World War II, Japan was taught by Americans to compete not in quantity but in quality. What was driving Japan's productivity up while America's stalled was the use of *quality methods*. By eliminating mistakes and the need to rework or repair things, Japanese plants were getting more product with less effort, and that is productivity.

In Japan, the highest award for quality is the Deming Prize, and its annual presentation ceremony is televised nationally in Japan. The award is for using the Deming quality philosophy, and from the 1950s, interest in the Deming Prize helped to spread that philosophy across Japan.

After the war, the Japanese were desperate to rebuild their economy and were willing to learn and change and try new ways of thinking. It may have been a sense of national desperation that spread the philosophy so quickly. The nation's geographic limitations and its homogeneous population may have helped. But whatever caused Japan's economic success, corporate winners of the Deming Prize are all but guaranteed continuing financial success.

What the Deming Prize had done for Japan helped to get a quality award in the United States.

In preparation for the Reagan White House Conference on Productivity, several subcommittees were formed to study what could be done to solve the productivity problem. One of them, with David Kearns of Xerox as chairman, was to consider the possibility of a national award for productivity improvement. Tribus, who knew Kearns from their work together at Xerox, asked to be on that subcommittee, and Kearns agreed. By rewriting the award proposal, Tribus, who had studied the Deming

Prize, changed the emphasis from productivity to quality. No one else on the subcommittee opposed the change so long as there was something concrete that could be measured. "To many people," Tribus says, "quality remains an intangible, unmeasurable characteristic." To the degree that he could, Tribus tried to make the proposed National Quality Award more like the Deming Prize.

The first problem was to make any award a reality. Tribus says Meese vetoed the award recommendation, saying that government had no business giving awards. "Government is not the solution," Reagan had said two years earlier, and in his White House, that wasn't a slogan, it was the Nicene Creed. People who would later work in Congress on the award said that more than any other administration in recent memory Reagan had "ideologues" rather than experts in major posts. Jim Turner, the staff director with the House Subcommittee on Technology and Competitiveness, recalls, "They also didn't understand what quality was." In 1983, not many people did, and the idea of a quality award went nowhere for more than two years, until an executive at a public utility got it moving again.

Chairman John Hudiburg of Florida Power & Light in Miami went to Representative Don Fuqua (D-Fla.), who was chairman of the House Committee on Science and Technology, to persuade him that quality was giving the economic edge to Japan, and a national quality award would help combat that. In January 1986, Fuqua sent Turner to Florida Power & Light to look at what was being done there with a quality method. Six years later, Turner still remembered vividly the enthusiasm of the people there that persuaded him that a quality method was not a "flavor of the month" management improvement program. Fuqua went to Japan to see how the Deming Prize worked. "If you didn't have the example of the Deming Prize in Japan," Turner says, "I doubt you'd ever have had a quality award here." In the summer of 1986, more as a service to Hudiburg than anything else, Fuqua introduced a bill to establish a national quality award. There were hearings in the House, but the bill went nowhere. At the end of that term, Fuqua retired after twenty-four years in the House, eight as chairman of the Committee on Science, Space, and Technology.

His fight was taken up in the next Congress by Representative Doug Walgren (D-Pa.) for an entirely personal reason. "He [Fuqua] was a favorite of mine," Walgren says, "somebody I liked very much." He thought of the quality award proposal as an honor to Fuqua. Walgren chaired the Subcommittee on Science, Research, and Technology that held hearings on the Fuqua proposal in 1986 and the redrafted proposal in 1987. Hudiburg was the lead witness both years, and he laid out what he thought the award should be. "First," he said, "it should be prestigious." He wanted the president to present it. "Second, I think the award should be self-funding." He didn't want tax money used. "Third, and the core of the whole thing, the award must be won the old-fashioned way, it must be earned."

Other witnesses at the first hearings in 1986 included Tribus, then director of the Center for Advanced Engineering Study at MIT,* and Dr. Joseph Juran, head of the Juran Institute, one of the country's leading quality

· · · · · · · · ·

* Tribus has had successful careers in industry, government, education, consulting, and he is now working in experimental energy.

consulting firms. In 1987, because of other commitments, he sent his written statement of support with a vice president from his institute.

In the Congress, there was no active opposition. When the bill was sent from committee to the full House, it carried an endorsement from Commerce Secretary Malcolm Baldrige, who was pleased that "the President's own theme of 'The Quest for Excellence' [will be] the medal's inscription." The award went through the House and Senate quickly and without opposition, partly because no one wanted to vote against quality, but mostly because of the staff work that had been done to make sure nothing went wrong. Walgren says, "It was a natural politically. It cost nothing, it was mainstream, and it was probusiness." The only foreseeable snag was at the White House, where the president who would have to sign it into law wanted government out of business.

Even though Walgren had introduced the bill to honor Don Fuqua, he didn't try to have the award named for Fuqua. It was not a reasonable political expectation. "If you're lucky," he says, "you get your name on a federal building in your district, not on a national award." It was, however, the name on the national award that probably got the bill signed by Reagan.

Commerce Secretary Baldrige was a close friend of Ronald Reagan's, and they would go horseback riding together. Baldrige was also an amateur rodeo contestant. He was born in Omaha, Nebraska, in 1922, but Baldrige was not some dirt-poor ranch hand. His father had been a member of Congress, and Malcolm was a graduate of Yale with a degree in English. However, he had earned his own success. He had worked his way up from a foundry hand at an iron mill to president of the company in thirteen years. As a student one summer, he worked on a Nebraska ranch, where he picked up the skill of calf roping, one of many events in a classic rodeo. He never gave it up, and his admiration of cowboys was well known. Asked why he enjoyed the company of cowboys, he said, "They don't talk unless they have something to say." (Whether it was that admiration for the taciturn or his education in the language, Baldrige fought a losing battle to make the thirty-eight thousand Commerce employees write in straightforward English. That effort ought to have won him an award, but it didn't.) He was the Professional Rodeo Man of the Year in 1980 and was elected to the National Cowboy Hall of Fame in 1984.

Rodeo killed him on Saturday, July 25, 1986.

He was practicing in Walnut Creek, California, for a rodeo when his horse reared and fell on him. The saddle horn may have hit the huge belt buckle that was his fa-vorite—rodeo riders usually wear belt buckles the size of Montana—but whatever happened, doctors could not stop the bleeding from massive abdominal injuries. As his blood pressure fell from the loss of blood, his heart stopped. He was sixty-four.

On Thursday, August 5, 1986, on the floor of the U.S. Senate, the already-passed House Bill 812 to establish the National Quality Award was amended to read "the Malcolm Baldrige National Quality Award." It was the only amendment to the act in either chamber. Senator Ernest F. Hollings (D-S.C.) told his Senate colleagues, "Secretary Baldrige will be sorely missed. I believe this bill is a fine way to recognize both the man and the values that he expressed so well." The president signed the bill on August 20, 1986, less than two weeks after its final passage in Congress.

In official Washington, it is generally accepted as fact that if the bill had not carried the name of Malcolm Baldrige so the president could honor his old friend, Reagan would not have signed it. Whether that is true is beside the point; it is *believed* to be true, and that is enough. "The bill would never have seen the light of day," Tribus says, "if Doug Walgren hadn't been smart enough to see that that was the only way you'd get it past the president." Walgren, however, says it wasn't his idea. He says that it came from someone in the Commerce Department, but he can't remember who. Neither can Turner. Whoever had the flash of genius that got the Malcolm Baldrige National Quality Award over its last perceived hurdle is unknown to us.

Before the bill could move through the Congress, its sponsors had to be able to say who would administer the award. Put it in the hands of the wrong agency, and it could become a political award or a popularity contest. If it was to have any value, then Hudiburg's third requirement—the award must be earned—had to be not only true but obvious. Like Caesar's wife, the Baldrige Award had to be above suspicion. After considering several possible homes for the administration of the award, Walgren, Turner, and others settled without much enthusiasm on the Department of Commerce and its agency, the National Bureau of Standards, later renamed the National Institute of Standards and Technology. (We like the old name much better, but for consistency, we'll use the new name or its acronym throughout.)

Created by Congress in 1901, NIST's job is basic scientific research and defining physical measurements. If that doesn't sound interesting or important, imagine how impossible daily life would be if every gas station could decide how much gas was in a gallon, if every fabric store could say how much cloth was in a yard, and if every manufacturer could determine what size its AA battery should be. NIST sets measurement standards and creates new and more accurate ways to measure, which explains why it developed the first atomic clock to measure time in billionths of a second.

The agency's work is scientific and technological, not political, and the agency in 1987 was considered somewhat drab and a bit of a political backwater. It was also considered thoroughly honest and unbiased, and in the world's scientific community, it is not only respected, it is admired. If the idea was to develop objective measurements for the Malcolm Baldrige National Quality Award, what better agency than the National Institute of Standards and Technology, whose whole existence was defined by standards and measurements? Even Deming, no fan of the Baldrige Award, conceded, "At least they put it in the right place."

The job to develop the criteria was given to Curt Reimann, who had joined the agency as a research chemist in 1962, the year after he got his doctorate from the University of Michigan. He has held increasingly important positions at the agency and has won the Rank Award, the highest award in the government's Senior Executive Service. Tribus describes him as "a very savvy guy; really, a wonderful man." In the spring of 1987, he had kept up with the award bill's progress in Congress and was working on possible concepts that might be useful for the quality award. He went to work in earnest when it was named for Baldrige and seemed certain to win approval. Reimann was told in late September that incoming Secretary of Commerce C. William Verity, Jr., a former chairman of the President's Task Force on Private Initiative, wanted President Reagan to present the first awards, which meant they would have to be presented the next year, 1988. The pace to develop the criteria became frantic—seven-day, eighty-hour weeks.

Reimann says he talked to "scores of people." The four experts—Deming, Juran, Philip B. Crosby, and Dr. Armand V. Feigenbaum, a quality expert since the 1940s—were consulted in September and early October. Juran and Feigenbaum liked the idea; Deming and Crosby did not. Deming declined to participate in any award that was not based on his philosophy. Crosby would later write that the award was "potentially as destructive to business as deregulation was to the savings and loan industry."

Even while acknowledging that problems are possible, the people who worked to make the Baldrige Award a reality like what is happening. Walgren says he and others who worked on the bill didn't anticipate how the award "would be absorbed and given a life of its own" by private industry. Turner says that after only two years, the popularity and acceptance of the Baldrige Award was at the level he thought it would be in ten years.

It continues to have presidential support. President George Bush personally awarded the Baldrige prize three times during his four years in office; the other year, he was tied up with the Persian Gulf War. Officials expect that President Bill Clinton will present the 1993 awards, and the cover of the *1993 Award Criteria* carries a quote that he provided: "Continued emphasis on quality by American companies is critical. It is what makes 'Made in the USA' something to be proud of." Clinton is familiar with quality systems in government. Arkansas had an active and growing quality movement when he was governor, and he's interested in the problem of productivity growth. In a speech in July 1993, he told an audience in Chicago, "Productivity would go up dramatically" if every worker would read three books: *Leadership Is an Art, The Seven Habits of Highly Effective People,* and *Dr. Deming: The American Who Taught the Japanese About Quality.*

Every indication is that the president and Commerce Secretary Ron Brown will continue to support the Baldrige Award. Brown spoke to the award's annual Quest for Excellence meeting less than a month after the new administration took office. Theoretically, of course, the award could continue without presidential support, but there is no doubt that having the president make the awards guarantees publicity and prestige.

The Malcolm Baldrige National Quality Award was created by Congress and could be killed by Congress, but there is not even a hint that Congress is considering that. In fact, the 103rd Congress is considering a bill to remove the restriction that limits each category to only two winners. If it passes, the Baldrige Award could be given to as many manufacturing, small business, and service companies as deserved it. Perhaps a more important feature of the bill is that it will create a Baldrige Award in education. As of this writing, the bill has passed the House and is awaiting action in the Senate. At the National Institute of Science and Technology, where the education award is being studied, another effort is under way that could expand the Baldrige Award to health care as well.

The Malcolm Baldrige National Quality Award needs the goodwill of Congress to continue. It also needs the support of the business community. All it costs the government are a few salaries at NIST, which are not enough in the federal budget even to be noticed. The Baldrige

Award program is paid for by an endowment fund, provided by industry, and the application fees—at least $1,200 for small companies, $4,000 for large ones, plus other fees for site visits and written section reviews. The number of applications and criteria printed and distributed (or copied and unofficially distributed by companies) has remained high, but the number of formal applications for the award has dropped slightly for a variety of apparently temporary economic reasons. Another reason might be that company executives are learning that it takes years to get a quality system in place before companies can even consider applying for the Baldrige Award. The other possibility is that as more states use the Baldrige criteria to establish state awards, companies are applying for their state award first, perhaps as a practice for a national application.

As long as the prestige of winning outweighs the cost and trouble of applying, the Malcolm Baldrige National Quality Award's future will be secure. However, the award has not yet reached the goal that the original supporters of it set when they were fighting for the bill—"to have a quality award in the United States that was as important as the Deming award in Japan."

8

. . . . .

Education and Health Care

I pay the schoolmaster, but 'tis the schoolboys
that educate my son.
—Ralph Waldo Emerson

The owners at Zytec, the Baldrige Award winner, adopted the Baldrige quality management system not because they thought it would be easy or fun, but because they believed it was necessary to stay in business. The incentive was survival. Even in the power supply industry known then for its mediocrity, sooner or later, by accident, luck, normal variation, or business intent, some company would have become a little less mediocre and taken away Zytec's unhappy customers. The choice for the company was quality or quit. There was no one to bail them out if they got it wrong.

Now let's imagine what might have happened if Zytec had been guaranteed increasing amounts of financing, not just company security but an expanding payroll, especially among managers, and a steady supply of customers no matter how unresponsive, unhappy, or resentful those customers might be. If times got tight, the customers could be given less; if they wanted to get as much as they once had, they'd have to pay more for it. Some high-powered commission would study Zytec's performance, report that it was just horrible, then pour money into the company to improve it. Ten years later that commission or another like it would do the same thing over again, even if no improvements had been made the first time and the customers were by now surly, rebellious, and in some cases violent.

If a business is guaranteed survival no matter how awful it becomes, there is no economic reason for the owners to put themselves through the difficulty and upset of changing, even if changing means improving. The only reason something might be done would be some individual owner's belief that there had to be a better way.

Welcome to the world of public education.

In April 1983, the National Commission on Excellence in Education delivered its sixty-four-page report on public education, "A Nation at Risk." The report concluded that public education in the United States was being destroyed by "a rising tide of mediocrity that threatens our very future as a Nation and a people." In what seems a bit of hyperbole to make a point, the commissioners wrote, "If an unfriendly foreign power had attempted to impose on America the mediocre educational performance that exists today, we might well have viewed it as an act of war."

A week later, the National Task Force on Education for Economic Growth concluded, "Our schools are not doing an adequate job of educating for today's requirements in the workplace, much less tomorrow's." That made sense to many Americans who were, at about that time, becoming concerned that the United States was not doing well economically in international competition.

Suddenly, school reform was politically popular, as parents demanded a better education for their children. In *High School*, a book published in 1983, Dr. Ernest L. Boyer, president of the Carnegie Foundation for the

Advancement of Teaching, began his prologue with this optimistic paragraph:

> Education is in the headlines once again. After years of shameful neglect, educators and politicians have taken the pulse of the public school and found it faint. Concern for the health of public education, stirred by a spate of new studies, offers fresh hope that in the years ahead we'll be able to adopt a serious, coherent plan for school reform. Getting the public's attention always has been the first step in the march toward progress in our nation.

But there was no march toward progress. In the intervening ten years, public schools in the United States have gotten worse, not better. In every decade since the 1940s, there has been at least one major study of American public education, and all of them concluded that public education was bad and getting worse. Despite the money that has been poured into public education, despite the new regulations and requirements, despite the hard work and sacrifice of teachers and principals, despite the anguish of students and the anger of their parents, despite the sometimes bizarre experiments and social fiddling that followed each report, the fact is that public education in America is not organized to produce quality and, therefore, it cannot produce quality.

For public education to improve, the system has to be changed from quantity to quality thinking, and until it is, no number of commission reports or legislative reforms will make it better. The basic problem with "A Nation at Risk" was that it did not recognize the systemic problem, so it recommended solutions designed to improve parts of the public education system, but not to transform the system. In effect, the report recommended hiring more inspectors and giving them better testing tools. To say it again: Inspection doesn't produce quality; testing doesn't produce education.

In schools where a quality management system has been tried, it has made an enormous difference. In 1991 in *Quality or Else*, we reported on Mount Edgecumbe High School in Sitka, Alaska, perhaps the best known of the quality success schools.

George Westinghouse Vocational and Technical High School is as unlike Mount Edgecumbe as a school could be. Mount Edgecumbe is a public *boarding* school with 160 or so students in a pleasant, if often rainy, town of 7,000 people. Westinghouse had 1,759 students in the fall of 1992 and is in downtown Brooklyn, New York, a couple of blocks from the East River, tucked away on Johnson Street between the entrance and exit ramps for the Brooklyn and Manhattan bridges. Within a few blocks are federal, state, and family courts. The area now is primarily business and industrial, but there is some residential property, including the Fort Greene Public Housing Project. Until the mid-1980s, the neighborhood was a collection of aging or empty storefronts. These were razed for Metrotech, a public-private development with a college, a bank, and a public service company surrounding the school.

The four-story school building is typical institutional architecture. There's an older Gothic section, built in 1906 of gray stone. It used to have Depression-era Works Project Administration (WPA) murals on the auditorium wall, but they were destroyed in a renovation. The main entrance is through a newer section built in 1963 of vanilla-colored brick. On either side of the concrete walk to the main entrance, a teacher and some students have planted flower gardens and trees. To the right of the entrance are two other trees, planted in remembrance of two students who were killed in their neighborhoods. In 1991, a student was paralyzed from the waist down when he was shot inside the building by an intruder.

That explains the security system inside the doors that all students must pass through, the X-ray machines that check their book bags and purses, and a third machine that randomly selects students for a more thorough search with hand-held metal detectors. Armed students exist even in smaller towns, but it's far more common in inner-city schools, like Westinghouse. (Weapons seem particularly prevalent in New York City, which now has a school security force of 2,600, more cops than a medium-sized city.)

Officially, the school is open to any student in New York City, but 85 percent of the students are from Brooklyn. The student body is about 75 percent black, 22 percent Latino, 2 percent Asian, and 1 percent white. The school began as an all-male institution and did not admit females until the 1970s. It remains overwhelmingly male.*

The students have the usual inner-city problems. Most are from single-parent, low-income homes; about half qualify for the free-lunch program. Many arrive at Westinghouse with little or no motivation, a history of failure, low self-esteem, poor math and reading skills; and most of them will be the first in their families to graduate from high school—if they graduate. The surprise is that

• • • • • • • • • •

* The Quality Steering Committee is now working on a program to recruit more female students.

despite the problems, more students will graduate from Westinghouse than from most other New York City high schools. The dropout rate at Westinghouse is about 5 percent, not quite a third of the city average, and that's after not quite three years of a quality program that started at the top.

Lewis A. Rappaport took over as principal in the fall of 1986 after Westinghouse had gone through seven principals in nine years. Rappaport wanted the job "because I saw the possibility of turning this school, which was the best-kept secret in Brooklyn, into an institution that really had a good reputation and deserved wider recognition." In 1987, Franklin P. Schargel, his longtime friend and colleague—they met as teachers in 1965—came aboard as an assistant principal. Neither man knew anything about a quality system in education, but in 1988, as part of a business outreach program, the two men attended a quality seminar led by National Westminster Bank USA. After twenty-five staff and thirty-four students attended other National Westminster seminars, a bank trainer went to the school to teach the entire staff.

Schargel heard more about quality in education at an American Society for Quality Control meeting at Fordham University, and in the fall of 1990, he went to a Boston seminar on quality in education. "There was a workshop delivered by Larrae Rocheleau, who is superintendent of Mount Edgecumbe," Schargel says, "and I heard Larrae and could not believe what I was hearing. He was an educator who was enthusiastic and who was going to make dramatic changes and had started to make dramatic changes in this small school in Sitka, Alaska. I met Larrae after the workshop, and I said, 'You've got to tell more.' " Schargel credits Rocheleau with going out of his way to help, explaining how the system worked, recommending books and magazines to read and videotapes to watch.

Rappaport remembers Schargel's phone call when he got back from Boston. " 'I've found it, I've found it,' " he [Schargel] said. I said, 'What have you found?' He said, 'I've found the answer to all the things we've been talking about, and it finally starts making sense. We've got a process, there's a system, there's the philosophy, there's everything.' " Saturday, when both men were off, they met at a diner on Long Island and Schargel explained what he'd learned in Boston and Rappaport's part in it. "If this system is going to work," Schargel said, "you're going to have to buy into it. Otherwise, forget it . . . it's out of the question." This was in keeping with the quality system developed by Deming, who insists that quality can only come from the top, and if the top executive won't do it, it won't get done. Rappaport agreed to do it—on the condition that Schargel take over as quality coordinator.

On January 30, 1991, Rappaport stood in front of a faculty meeting, and, as Schargel remembers, said, "What we're doing at Westinghouse isn't working. I am in charge of the education at Westinghouse, so it's my fault. I need your help to make it work." He talked about Total Quality Management. To persuade a skeptical staff that this was not the latest flavor-of-the-month educational fad, he promised them, "As long as I am principal, this school will use TQM techniques and tools to address the challenges which we face."

The Westinghouse quality program does not strictly follow the Deming management system. It does, however, use the 14 Points, so the first thing the staff did was answer the questions "What are we doing, and why are we doing it?" To satisfy the need for constancy of purpose, the staff wrote a mission statement.

> The purpose of George Westinghouse Vocational and Technical High School is to provide quality vocational, technical and academic educational programs which will maximize each student's full potential in today's changing technological society and prepare students to meet the challenges of our rapidly changing world. In an era of intense international competition, each student will be prepared to meet the demands of the world of work, post-secondary education and address life's challenges.

The faculty had to be trained in quality methods, problems had to be identified and arranged by priority, and skeptics had to be won over, not all at once, but in good time. Some skeptics were won over by almost immediate results. By using quality methods, the school reduced the number of students cutting classes by nearly 40 percent in six weeks. Most dramatic was the response of the poorest-performing students. In January 1991, Schargel and Rappaport found 151 students who had failed every course they took. In June, only 11 students still failed everything.

Westinghouse is one of more than a hundred regular high schools in New York City, and while it can control its own system to some degree, it has no control over the expanded system in which it exists. The New York City school bureaucracy insists that every child have a letter grade for every class—"Incomplete" is not allowed. That grade is fed into a computer that prints out traditional report cards. "The computer," Schargel says, "programs kids for failure." Students do not "fail" at Westinghouse in the traditional sense. Some take longer than others to succeed, but they do not fail. When Westinghouse students are promoted, it is because they have earned the promotion. This is opposite to the New York City Board of Education's "age-appropriate placement" policy, meaning students are promoted because of their age or "time served" rather than their competence.

Since September 1992, every student at Westinghouse has signed a contract. It had originally been written by the faculty and was rewritten for 1993–94 with help from students. The contract is one page and spells out clearly and exactly what is required from each student in seven specific areas—grades, attendance, preparation, class participation or shop/class work, homework, exams, and decorum. To assure that teaching is consistent enough to help the students, each teacher must return to each student at least ten graded homework assignments and three tests each grading period.

To make the students understand that school is for learning, the contract prohibits radios, beepers (the technology of choice for teenage drug dealers), eating, drinking, or chewing gum, abusive language, graffiti on desks and walls, and wearing hats indoors (with an exception for religious requirements). At the beginning of the quality program, faculty and staff said unless the tone of the school could be improved, nothing would get better, and that led to the contract paragraph on decorum. To an outside visitor, it seems to have worked, with just enough youthful rebellion thrown in to keep life interesting. Told they couldn't wear hats indoors, some students initially switched to visors and headbands. No lawyer on earth understands the concept of "the letter of the law" as well as your average teenager.

Perhaps the most interesting quality change is the Apprentice Training Program.

The highest dropout rate at Westinghouse and at other high schools across the country is in the ninth grade, when fourteen- and fifteen-year-old students are suffering teenage angst, raging hormonal storms, and fear of an entirely new school environment where they are at the bottom of the social and scholastic order. High school teachers don't like ninth-grade classes because the students generally are more unruly and usually unprepared. At Westinghouse now, every ninth-grade student is paired with a junior or senior student, who is then partially responsible for the younger student's education.

The apprentice program was first suggested by two teachers, Sal Giovaniello and William Downes. They taught seniors, and the idea of using the seniors to help the ninth graders seemed reasonable. They took the apprentice idea to Rappaport expecting that he would shoot it down, as school principals traditionally shoot down innovative ideas from teachers. Instead, he told them to test their idea, as would be required in any quality program in manufacturing. They did, trying it in their own senior classes.

By the end of the test, more material had been taught, scores had improved, and class attendance was up. One mother called and said if they took her son out of the apprentice program, she'd take him out of Westinghouse. Other teachers wanted their classes to take part, and student attitudes appeared to have improved dramatically, although attitude is all but impossible to measure objectively.

Giovaniello thinks the apprentice program helps ninth graders because "it eliminates most of the fear. It's like [having] a big brother or big sister. They feel more comfortable working with their own peers." Downes sees a payoff for the seniors as well. "They kind of feel like they're big shots, too," he says. "Here they are, they're acting as teachers and as big brothers." It helps the seniors review their own grasp of the material, because one of the best ways to learn anything is to have to teach it. Chris Zuniga, a senior, explained it as "a way of me giving something back, what I have learned from teachers. You know, it's like a chain reaction." Yaesang Sugrim, a senior, said, "You feel very good 'cause you feel like you helped somebody and made them learn something." George Zayas, another senior, said, "It's like teaching my little brother, so it gives me great satisfaction in teaching another person and making them leave this school knowing that they learned something."

Mark Gavoor sees another benefit. "They've got students mentoring students," he says, "and providing that support structure that maybe twenty or thirty years ago was there for everybody from a family structure standpoint, and I think it's very exciting." Gavoor is from Colgate-Palmolive, one of the school's business partners. Sherwood Bliss of IBM, another partner, says Westinghouse is different from other schools he's been to. "The kids are more self-disciplined," he says. "They seem to have a much greater sense of purpose, and the intellectual curiosity here is just terrific." Ray Peters, who teaches business machine technology likes the apprentice program because "the seniors act more responsible, and the ninth-graders act less immature, so it's a good atmosphere . . . because everybody seems to be serious about why they're here."

Students are no longer expected merely to listen to

lectures and do as they are told. Their opinions count, and they are part of the system, helping to decide what they'll learn and how they'll learn it. "They came up with their own grading criteria," Jeanne Benecke, a math teacher, says of her students. "They also decided that they want an exam every two weeks; they also decided that they want a quiz every Tuesday. It's totally driven by them, which is new for me, but it's also exciting because now they want to do it. They *want* to do this work." In the past, she says, she was taught that she was the one with all the knowledge and all the power and all the control. She no longer believes that. "They have the knowledge," she says, "and my job is to guide them to find it. . . . I'm no longer the one who's giving anything. I'm just guiding."

One way she guided recently was to get students to write at the top of their test papers how long each had studied for it. When the papers were graded and returned, the students used a graph to correlate hours studied and grades received. Those who had studied longer did better. If you're about to say, "Everyone knows that," no, everyone doesn't. Many parents were surprised to learn that their children would have to master skills in order to graduate, and for them and their children the correlation between hours of study and grades earned is an insight.

Rappaport says that active involvement of students in their own education is one of the significant changes that a continual improvement quality system creates. Such involvement runs all the way to the principal's office. In the old days, the principal gave orders, and the teachers obeyed. He doesn't do that anymore. "If you want to find out the best way to do things," he says, "you go to the people who are most affected—the students, the parents, the teachers. They'll tell you how." One of the successes of which Rappaport is most proud is the involvement of parents in the quality program. A few of them have even volunteered to take a weekend quality training course taught by IBM experts. Membership in the Parent-Teacher Association has increased, the group is far more active than it used to be, and there is a Quality Steering Committee that includes parents, students, and staff. Schargel says that the steering committee now "drives" the quality program at the school.

Westinghouse is run for the customers—students, parents, and staff on the inside; colleges and businesses on the outside. Businesses in the community were asked how Westinghouse graduates could be better prepared. They said the young people needed better speaking skills, so a mandatory speech class was added in the junior year. When the school asked a neighborhood college what it wanted, the college said it needed incoming students with better Scholastic Aptitude Test scores. Rappaport and Schargel pointed out that their students could not afford private SAT review courses, so the college agreed to provide college students as tutors for the high school.* It is a classic business-supplier relationship, where each helps the other succeed.

Ricoh Corporation, another business partner, maintains a similar relationship with Westinghouse High School. The Japanese copier manufacturer provides spare parts, training, and supplies for the copier repair courses.

◆ ◆ ◆ ◆ ◆ ◆ ◆ ◆ ◆ ◆

* Many Americans who admire the Japanese education system do not realize the importance of private, often expensive "cram schools" that Japanese students routinely attend to learn how to take and pass entrance tests.

It gets in return highly qualified potential employees. Wayne A. Mize of Ricoh says, "What we're hoping to do through the quality process is introduce the concept of continuous quality improvement . . . and instill proper ways of, as an example, electronic troubleshooting, so when they come to Ricoh and are looking for work, they're already qualified. . . . You shouldn't have to re-work, or reeducate, or retrain people coming out of schools." That relationship started after Ricoh officials toured the school and told Schargel, "The [quality] process that you are running is correct."

The United Federation of Teachers, the powerful local of the American Federation of Teachers, apparently agrees. Schargel quotes the school's union chapter leader, Michael Graff, as saying: "I'm skeptical. I will always be skeptical. The only thing I know is that the process works."

Not only does a quality management system work in a school, whether it's Westinghouse High School or a university, but it works *for less money.* The object of a quality system is not only to produce quality, but to produce it at a reasonable cost. "The budget of New York City in education," Rappaport says, "was cut seven hundred fifty million dollars in the past two years, so not only are we doing the same with less money, we are doing *more* with less money." In the last five years, enrollment at Westinghouse has gone up slightly, but the faculty has been cut 21 percent because of budget cuts. "Total quality education," Rappaport says, "is not more expensive."

In contrast, public education using the traditional quantity management system is increasingly more expensive, and that increasing expense is likely to cause more public policy confrontations. Taxpayers, sick of paying more and getting less, are voting against school bonds, causing bitterness among educators, who feel themselves squeezed, underpaid, and unappreciated, stuck in a system over which they have no control. It is tough to tell a teacher who hasn't had a raise in years that putting more money into education won't make it better. However, a five-year experiment by the Annie E. Casey Foundation that ended in June 1993 had poured money into public schools in four cities; there were no significant improvements. Other tests and studies have shown similar results; still, an official of the National Education Association, another teachers' union, is quoted in a 1993 magazine article as saying, "Students are threatened only by the failure of policymakers to give education the money it deserves." How much would that be?

We can get a hint, perhaps, from the cost of a public college education. Between 1980 and 1990, according to one report, median family income went up 73 percent, but public college costs went up 109 percent. Only two items went up more—medical care was up 117 percent, and *private* college education, up 146 percent. Even if there were no other benefits (but there are), the case for quality management in education is compelling as a matter of economics.

And it can be done.

Rappaport says each school must first adapt a quality system to its own culture, "but certainly by applying the process, by a commitment of leadership to the process, by having steering committees . . . by having a vision and a mission statement, and by realizing that a continuous improvement process is not a quick fix, and being in it for the long haul and not as something which we're going to get into today and be done with tomorrow . . . yes, it can be done in schools throughout the country." Schargel agrees, but warns that a successful quality system cannot be copied. Again, he is lavish in his praise for the people from Mount Edgecumbe who helped him, but "you cannot copy their materials. Our culture is different from their culture, our tastes are different, our inputs are different, our outcomes are different. . . . You've got to change . . . and you've got to be willing to adapt. The people who are looking for a template that they can impose over their system are doomed to fail." Both men are adamant that, difficult though it may be, a quality management system can be adapted to any school anywhere.

"What we're doing here at Westinghouse," Rappaport says, "can be done at other schools." His students come from neighborhoods where gunfire is a nightly occurrence, and most of them learn the etiquette of funerals early in life. Rappaport says he thinks about fifty students have died since he took over in 1986. He doesn't keep statistics handy; it is too depressing. He does know that some of the students come to Westinghouse because, with the student contract on decorum and with the security system—paid for by the city, but the school's business partners said they'd do it if the city didn't—it is safer than other New York high schools. Think of that: American teenage students pick a high school not because of its location, reputation, or curriculum, but because they may actually survive four years in it. "If we can succeed here," Rappaport says, "it can be done all over America."

◆ ◆ ◆ ◆ ◆

We have never met anyone who was opposed to reform in education, so long as all the other people did the reforming. The only other area of America of which we are aware where that is equally true is health care. No one involved in the profession seems happy with it. The data are well known. The United States ranks first among the nations of the world in health costs, twelfth among developed nations in life expectancy, and twenty-first in infant mortality. In 1991, the United States pumped more than 13 percent of its gross domestic product into health care, while no other nation spent as much as 10 percent. The cost to Americans is staggering. The Ford Motor Company now spends more on health care than on steel. Some Americans go to Mexico or Canada to buy their prescription drugs because the same drugs cost less than they do in the United States.

According to a public opinion poll, Americans think health care specialists make too much money, yet increasingly American doctors are saying the money isn't worth the aggravation. They are retiring early, blaming government paperwork, insurance company interference, and malpractice lawsuits.

Everyone involved says that health care has to change, but there is very little agreement on what should change, how it should change, and who should pay for it.

In 1987, Dr. Deming was hospitalized near his home in Washington, D.C., with phlebitis in his right leg. (In later seminars, he told students that he had a problem in "my right hind hoof.") During his hospital stay, he made observations and kept notes about what went on, good and bad.* Most of the time, he was forced to lie in bed

◆　◆　◆　◆　◆　◆　◆　◆　◆　◆

* Continuing the habit we first noticed in his private travel journals, dating back to the late 1940s, Deming is most eloquent when describing food he particularly enjoyed. Of this hospital he wrote, "The food is superb," then went into salivary detail.

with his leg elevated, so the observations are almost exclusively of what happened to him, one patient in one relatively brief stay. He wrote a paper from his notes in September 1987 that was published in the Spring 1990 issue of the *Journal of the Society for Health Systems*.*

If you read his notes and think about a manufacturing plant, everything he wrote could apply to assembling automobiles or television sets. The notes describe a factory—in this case, a health-care factory—that is out of control. After a particularly grievous mistake by a nurse, Deming's doctor "assured me that he is running this lapse down in every detail, and that nothing like it will ever happen again here—the usual supposition: working on only an actual defect, not on its cause." To repeat a lesson from the Red Bead Experiment, no one inside a system can produce more quality than the system is organized to produce. Deming concluded that the hospital supervisor was not using a quality management system, that doctors and nurses could not change the system that was being used, and, therefore, everything that had gone wrong for him would continue to go wrong for others. There is no doubt that he was right.

However, of all the things that Deming observed going wrong, not one had anything to do with the cost of care, which is the federal government's major concern. The mistakes had nothing to do with a lack of insurance, or choice of doctors or hospital, or cost of drugs, or anything else currently being publicly discussed under the

◆　◆　◆　◆　◆　◆　◆　◆　◆

* The notes were excerpted by Mary Walton in her book *Deming Management at Work* and reprinted in full by Cecelia Kilian in her *World of W. Edwards Deming* (2nd ed.).

general heading "Health-Care Reform." At this writing, no one debating reform has said in public that what is generally wrong in health care is the lack of a quality management system. If a quality system were used, many, perhaps even most, of those other problems would be corrected. It is certain, for instance, that costs would come down. The current estimate is that a service industry without quality management—and that describes most of the health-care industry in the United States—will waste 25 to 40 percent of its budget. On current estimates, that would represent about $225 billion to $360 billion in 1993.

Patrick Townsend and Joan Gebhardt, a husband and wife who work together as authors and quality consultants, say that what is going on now in health care closely parallels what American manufacturers went through in the 1980s searching for efficiency and effectiveness. The quality systems that manufacturers turned to, they say, will work equally well in health care.

In suggesting quality management systems for health-care companies, Townsend and Gebhardt use two examples—Intermountain Health Care with twenty-four facilities in Utah, Wyoming, and Idaho; and Froedtert Memorial Lutheran Hospital, a 284-bed teaching hospital in Milwaukee. In 1992, the "cost per case" at Intermountain facilities rose less than 3 percent, which was less than the rise in the average cost of living that year, and much less than the 10 to 12 percent increase in overall health costs that year.

In 1992, the cost of the quality program at Froedtert was $209,000, and part of that money was spent organizing and training employees on quality teams. Savings from a few of the ideas generated by those teams that year totaled $689,852, a net saving of nearly half a million dollars. The two consultants concluded, "Quality is a compelling goal for both ethical and financial reasons."

Paul Batalden, a medical doctor, heads the quality program for the Hospital Corporation of America (HCA) and walks around with a head full of quality health success stories, including ones on how to save money. At one of his hospitals, when doctors get lab reports on infections, each report lists the drugs that work to combat that infection. The list was always alphabetical. "One very creative pharmacist," Batalden says, "decided with the help of some physicians that we could list the drugs in order of increasing expense, so that the top drug that worked was also the best value. With that little change in the system, they were able to save two hundred fifteen thousand dollars in one hospital each year." A student of Deming, Batalden says, "Ways to reduce the cost in health care can be found in studying the system."

He says while doctors and nurses understand the idea of a system perfectly well—the human body is a system—"they lack the understanding of the way their work functions as a system." He learned of the importance of a system while looking down on cars being assembled in a Mazda plant. "One thing happened after another," he says. "People had to work together, it was clear. But then I realized why it was clear. I was standing on a catwalk. We don't have catwalks in hospitals." He says the flow diagram, the same type that Deming used in Japan in 1950, is critical in getting doctors to understand a quality management system.* "Health professionals," he says, "think of

• • • • • • • • • •

* The flow chart is figure 1 in chapter 2.

themselves as doing things, not making things." Once they accept that they make services, and they make information, then, Batalden says, they can think about who is the customer, who is the supplier, and what are the processes that can be improved.

The concept of improvement of the system is not part of medical training. What is important in medical training is the result, and if the result is correct, then how it was achieved must have been correct as well. Doris Quinn, nursing systems coordinator at Vanderbilt University and a consultant to HCA, says that medical mind-set leads to predictable behavior. If a medical student runs into a particular set of symptoms, orders five tests, then makes the correct diagnosis based on those test results, forevermore, when that doctor sees those symptoms, he or she will order the same five tests even if three of them can be shown to be unnecessary to the correct diagnosis.

If other doctors now copy the five-test example, and no one ever asks Deming's favorite question—By what method?—it is possible to imagine necessary tests not being done for other patients while labs do unnecessary tests for patients with those symptoms. The system would be out of control, which, in some cases, it clearly is. A doctor calling in to a radio talk show in Chicago in 1991 complained that at the hospital where he worked, getting a simple blood test done would require that more than a hundred people handle the blood sample.

Quinn from Vanderbilt has another example. During her own recent physical examination, she noticed a chart on the wall telling nurses the tests that each doctor wanted run for physicals. There was enormous variation from doctor to doctor. For the patient, that is immediately unsettling. Which tests are better? Would another doctor with a more extensive list of tests find something that my doctor will miss? Is my doctor running unnecessary tests that add to the cost? Why can't these people agree? Also, just having the list on the wall where patients can see it demonstrates that the doctors and nurses are more concerned with their own problems of supposed efficiency than they are with the patients' feelings. In any business but health care, those patients would be called customers, the people paying the bill.

That lack of customer concern may be one of the reasons for the change in relationships in medicine that Batalden has observed. He sees three distinct periods in medicine. Before 1700 it was largely a matter of hope, because doctors couldn't take a pulse reading until 1707, a blood pressure reading until 1726, or a temperature until 1730. Over the next 200 to 250 years, medicine became a matter of science, and, finally, "I think," he says, "about 1980 or so we began to see a new kind of pressure in health care. We began to see something that's hard for me to label." Before 1980, he says, patients would ask him what they should do, he would tell them, and they would say, "Thank you." After 1980, patients would ask him what they should do, he would tell them, and they would say, "Why?" "And I realized that what was new was a level of social accountability that was emerging." He thinks the shift may be as big as the previous shift from hope to science. "The good news," he says "is that the norms and standards that are changing open up a responsiveness to a new way of thinking about quality and improvement. I personally believe that that helps explain why this whole effort at systemic thinking about improvement is reaching such receptive ears today in health care."

The first step is to decide on the aim of the system.

What is health care supposed to do? Batalden thinks Americans expect too much. "People want to talk about optimum health, or people want to talk about the aim of medicine as well-being. There's a risk in that way of thinking, and that risk is that . . . the entire gross national product will be spent on health care." Batalden says everyone wants a cure, and sometimes a cure is not possible. "What has to be attended to," he says "is how to help people live their lives, how to help people restore their ability to function in daily society. . . . The need that patients and their families have is to limit the burden of illness on their lives. . . . reducing the cost of illness is a way of reducing the burden of illness on people's lives."

As an example, at Portsmouth Regional Hospital in New Hampshire, an HCA facility, orthopedic surgeons studied the system used in hip replacement surgery and found ways to get the patients back into society "more quickly, smoothly, and comfortably." First, the physical therapist joins the team sooner and has each patient practice the exercises before surgery so the patient knows what it feels like. Second, rather than let the patient feel pain, then ask for painkillers, the patient is mildly medicated and kept pain-free to speed recovery. Third, before the operation, hospital personnel check with the patient about his or her home: Would there be someone to help? Would the patient need convalescent care? Finally, as quickly as possible after the hip replacement operation, the patient goes into rehabilitation therapy. In all, Batalden says, "This reduced the length of their stay and reduced the trouble they encountered at home."

That addresses both the health needs of the customers and the personal and societal costs of illness. "But it doesn't go anywhere," he says, "unless you have knowledge of the system. So we get back to the same basic points about Profound Knowledge. Unless we understand that, we can't begin to improve [health care]."

The current health-care reform movement concerns him because he does not think the reformers have the right focus. "The people who wish to reform health care today, I think, would do well to remember that you improve health care by improving the degree to which the health care services match the needs that people have . . ." He says that when you understand the necessity of matching needs and services, you can make the aim of the health-care system clear and understandable to everyone. "That requires knowledge of the system as a means of production, and it's very difficult to have people sit still long enough to learn that." He says it is not only producing the service that matters, it's understanding how the service meets the need.

He talks about a group of obstetricians and gynecologists trying to learn why women who gave birth by caesarean section once always wanted it again, even if it wasn't medically necessary. The doctors looked at data to see if there were factors related to the baby, the mother, or the doctor, but they couldn't find any reason. When they asked the mothers, however, the women said they were having a second caesarean because *their* mothers had told them no other way was safe. That was once widely believed to be true.

What had happened, Batalden says, is that the doctors had created education programs for mothers and fathers about safe childbirth, "but they had left out the critical information resource." By studying the system, they found what was wrong. The mother's mother was included in the safe childbirth education program "so that she was able to give more reliable information." That simple solution to a complex and costly problem could only have been found through a stroke of luck, a brilliant insight, or the study of the system.

Other solutions are equally simple once you study the system. For instance, at Portsmouth, nurses handed food trays to patients, but nurses were often called away on more urgent duties, and the trays didn't get to the patients as they should have. By studying the complaints and the system of delivery, the hospital slightly reduced the number of nurses and hired more people in the dietary section to pass out the trays. Now the people responsible for the food were in direct contact with the customers. Customer complaints were taken seriously where before complaints had been considered nothing more than the spiteful work of "vicious nurses."

The hospital had been taking food service surveys among patients every six months. In the first survey after the change was made, the percentage of patients rating food service "excellent" went up 18 percent, a change unheard of in these surveys.

Batalden believes that health care can be transformed to a quality system, but not as it is being contemplated now. "We are not going to improve health care by laws," he says, "or by regulation or by inspection. We're going to improve health care when the leaders of health care can undertake the leadership of the improvement of health care." That is a restatement of Deming's belief that quality can only come from the top. Batalden says the top people in health care are beginning to recognize their responsibility.

In one sense, what is driving the change to quality management systems in the health care industry is exactly what drives it in manufacturing—survival. The whole system of health care in America is coming apart at the seams. Patients think doctors are insensitive and greedy, and doctors think medical decisions are being made by bureaucrats and insurance clerks. The federal government, trying to control costs, interferes with hospital administration, but costs continue to escalate. More people, mainly in medical administration, are hired to handle increasing paperwork, almost all of which is designed to cut costs. The Mayo Clinic has seventy full-time employees to answer questions about patient treatment and costs from twenty-four hundred insurance companies. Hospitals compete for patients with the latest expensive high-tech medical machine, often buying duplicate and wasteful equipment. "It isn't just whether we can get higher technology," Batalden says, "but it's whether we can apply that technology to reduce the burden of illness on people." That would be done if hospitals cooperated in technology and competed in concern for the patients. Since that isn't being done, other methods of control are increasingly being used. The North Carolina legislature in 1993 passed a law that prohibits health-care facilities from buying expensive new technology without the state's permission.

Lawsuits add their own expense to health care. Thomas Metzloff, a Duke University law professor, was quoted as saying that before 1970, the chance that a doctor would ever be sued for malpractice was "maybe one in twenty over an entire career." Now the odds are even, except in a high-risk specialty such as obstetrics, where the question is not whether you will be sued, but how many times you are sued and whether you can continue to afford liability insurance. One survey shows that 77 percent of obstetricians have been sued at least once and that four thousand of them quit practice every year.*

Federal and state governments and insurance companies create indescribable amounts of paperwork, insisting that patients, doctors, and hospitals fill out endless and repetitive forms, all of which are written in no known language. Imagine the savings if all those insurance and government health forms were replaced with a single form, written in English, that a high school graduate could complete. That requires nothing more than cooperation.

Hospitals have their own problem with forms. Dr. Joyce N. Orsini, an associate professor of management at Fordham University, tells the story of getting four copies of her hospital bill, all of which showed that she didn't owe anything. Why send them at all, she wondered, and even if there were a reason to send one, why send four? She checked.

The hospital administration wanted patients to get two bills—one to keep for personal records, one to return with payment. Orders were given: Send two copies. The person who was in charge of the computer that wrote bills programmed it to print two copies, but the person in charge of forms ordered duplicate-copy bills—print one, get two—only now the computer would print two, so you'd get four. Everyone had followed orders and done his or her best, but no one had asked, "By what method?"

Orsini also learned that 26 percent of the patients being billed in quadruplicate owed nothing, were not

♦   ♦   ♦   ♦   ♦   ♦   ♦   ♦   ♦   ♦

* A medical survey in New York found that the odds of a woman having a caesarean section are three times greater where malpractice suits are frequent and malpractice insurance premiums high.

going to send a payment back, and didn't need one bill, let alone four. A quarter of the time, effort, and expense of billing was totally wasted. Orsini says it took one hour of computer programming time to correct the problem and save all that wasted money.

Add it all together, and the lack of a quality management system in the health-care industry spells incredible amounts of money, and we haven't even mentioned the fraud and the known waste that the General Accounting Office says is out of control, adding at least 10 percent to the nation's health bill.

In one survey, consumers were asked to rate the best and worst buys among fifty ordinary items. Health-care managers and professionals will not be happy to learn that dentists and doctors were considered a poorer value than a used car, and the only thing that ranked lower in value than hospitals was pay-per-view television. "You see," Batalden says, "in a hospital, we have the very best pharmacy sitting right next to the very best laboratory, sitting right next to the very best X-ray department, sitting right next to the very best nursing department, and the hospital doesn't work." But it does have to be paid. As President Bill Clinton told Congress in February 1993, "All of our efforts to strengthen the economy will fail unless we take bold steps to reform our health-care system."

At this writing, Congress has not passed a health-care reform proposal. No matter what its final form, no one seems certain exactly how the proposed reform would work in detail. If the federal government used a quality management system, there would be a small test of the proposed reform—the "Do" of Plan-Do-Study-Act—to limit the damage should unexpected problems develop. Urgent though health-care reform is, one year of testing would not make it that much worse. Instead of a limited test, however, the federal government seems intent on what amounts to a universal test—nationwide adoption. The last time the government tried a universal test was in issuing the Susan B. Anthony dollar.

With or without a test, however, health care cannot be made to work by trying to patch a system that is out of control. Trying to do that is exactly what doctors did before 1700—slap a bandage on it and hope.

9

• • • • •

The Pentagon and the Press

> Life is not a spectacle or a feast;
> it is a predicament.
> —*George Santayana*

The beginning of the Cold War might reasonably be dated March 12, 1947, when President Harry Truman promised that the United States "would support free peoples who are resisting attempted subjugation by armed minorities or by outside pressures." It was a warning to the Soviet Union, which was then trying to take over Europe, not militarily but by subterfuge. It was a new kind of conflict for which there was not even a name. A month later, Bernard Baruch, the well-known American financier, told an audience in Columbia, South Carolina, "Let us not be deceived—we are today in the midst of a cold war." The conflict was named.*

The war's end could be dated November 9, 1989, the day East Germany finally gave up trying to keep its borders sealed and its citizens restricted. East Berliners went shopping in West Berlin in massive numbers, and the Berlin Wall, symbolically at that moment, ceased to exist. The Soviet Union had lost the Cold War.

• • • • • • • • • •

* The speech was written and the name coined by Herbert Bayard Swope, former editor of the defunct *New York World*. He won't be remembered; Baruch will. Life's like that.

In another sense, so had the United States Department of Defense.

An immediate and predictable result of the collapse of Communist regimes in Eastern Europe and the breakup of the Union of Soviet Socialist Republics, the "evil empire" itself, was a cut in the United States defense budget. From 1989 to 1993, the defense budget shrank by not quite 5 percent, which was the American "peace dividend." It doesn't sound like much until you realize that every other big-ticket item in the federal budget during that period increased by 19 to 116 percent. Nothing else declined. Every penny saved on defense was spent on something else, which may have influenced historian Paul Kennedy to observe in 1993 that "a reduction in defense expenditures may do little or nothing to assist a country's economic growth" unless the amount saved is wisely invested.

Whatever the government chooses to do with the money the military "saves," the Department of Defense still has to function effectively with less than it used to get. Those spending cuts have to come from somewhere, and the Department of the Navy is finding some of its share through a management approach, which started not as a way to save money but as a way to improve quality. The idea was to improve productivity at repair facilities, where defects were running as high as 4 percent all the time. The Navy calls its approach Total Quality Leadership; it is the quality management philosophy of Dr. W. Edwards Deming.*

◆ ◆ ◆ ◆ ◆ ◆ ◆ ◆ ◆ ◆

* For a detailed history of the quality movement in the Department of the Navy, see chapter 5 of *Deming Management at Work* by Mary Walton.

"The association with Dr. Deming's philosophy," explains Dan Howard, then under secretary of the navy, "really began at two places." He mentions the Navy Personnel Research and Development Center (NPRDC) in San Diego and the Naval Aviation Depot at Cherry Point, North Carolina. The idea for the quality program was born in 1981 when Dr. Laurie Broedling, a psychologist with NPRDC, went to a ninety-minute lecture by Deming expecting to hear about statistics, on which Deming is an expert. Instead, she heard about his management philosophy and later described herself as being "blown away" and "sold."

She sent another NPRDC psychologist, Dr. Steven Dockstader, to a seminar Deming gave in Boston. Dockstader and his colleague and wife, Dr. Linda Doherty, already knew about Deming. They had seen the network television documentary *If Japan Can . . . Why Can't We?* in June 1980. They were on vacation at the time with their two young children, heard a radio advertisement for the program as they drove along, and found a cheap motel with a black-and-white television set so they could watch. They were impressed with Deming but thought that he was dedicated to statistics. They had every right to believe that; they had been unintentionally misled.

And now, another hard turn onto the tangential highway so that we can make an overdue confession.

The people responsible for *If Japan Can . . .* were Reuven Frank, executive producer; Clare Crawford-Mason and Ray Lockhart, producers; Lloyd Dobyns, reporter-narrator; Dobyns and Frank, writers; and a ton of talented research and technical people. The program was highly honored and well received, particularly among industrialists and academics, and it introduced Deming to a much wider audience.

The two of us (C.C.-M. and L.D.) did the interviews with Deming, after Dr. Herbert Striner told us about him.* When Doherty and Dockstader watched the program in their motel room, they did not know that those of us doing the program did not understand what the Deming management philosophy was. Indeed, we did not understand that it was a philosophy. We knew that Deming was onto *something:* we did not know what that something was, and we had been unable to learn in repeated interviews. Even if we didn't understand it, we knew it was too important to leave out. A critic of *Fortune* magazine took us to task because we had not explained that Deming's method was statistical process control. We were concerned and upset to have missed that. When we started working more closely with Deming, we were childishly delighted to learn that the *Fortune* critic was completely wrong. We make no claim to level-headed maturity.

Back to the main road.

Broedling and the other enthusiasts at the Navy Personnel Research and Development Center at San Diego were across the bay from the North Island Naval Aviation Depot, one of six aviation repair facilities in the United States for the Navy and the Marine Corps.†

♦ ♦ ♦ ♦ ♦ ♦ ♦ ♦ ♦ ♦

* If you want the complete story, I wrote a four-page article in *SPC INK*, Fall 1992. It's the Statistical Process Control Newsletter from SPC Press, Inc., of Knoxville, Tennessee. (C.C.-M.)

†In 1993, three depots—Norfolk, Alameda, and Pensacola—were among military facilities the government ordered the Pentagon to close.

Dockstader and depot commanding officer Captain Phil Monroe agreed to run a controlled quality management test involving about five hundred people in one division.

A previous North Island commanding officer, Rear Admiral John Kirkpatrick, had just taken over as head of the Naval Aviation Logistics Center at Patuxent River, Maryland, so he was now in charge of all six aviation repair facilities. On a tour of the six, Kirkpatrick stopped last at North Island and was told about the planned test of the Deming quality management system. By the time the presentation ended, Kirkpatrick was sold—perhaps oversold. The planned one-division test at North Island became on his order an all-divisions policy at all six depots.

Just as in private industry, Kirkpatrick's motivation was survival. The small test at North Island would have taken a year or more, and there might not have been that much time before officials in Washington got even more fed up than they already were. Financial matters and bookkeeping throughout the Department of Defense are Byzantine on the best days, so exact comparisons are difficult to make. However, if the Naval Aviation Logistics Center had been a private business, it would have been $267 million in the hole and going deeper by the day when Kirkpatrick took over. There were several problems, but a basic one seemed to be poor quality. Kirkpatrick had never been happy with the quality of depot work, not when he was in charge of North Island and even less as North Island's customer in the Pacific Fleet. He was willing to take the responsibility to try to improve it. By January 1985, he and his top people had worked out a plan and began sending people to Deming's four-day quality seminars.

Kirkpatrick went to his first seminar later that year. His quality coordinator, Wayne Putnam, said he had to, that if he was going to lead, he had to understand. Even eight years later, Kirkpatrick remembers the first day being so painful that he wanted to leave. He stayed when an aide reminded him that he had 260 people under his command in the room. If he walked out, the quality program was dead. On the second day, "the light went on." By the end of the fourth day, when the seminar ended, Kirkpatrick was so impressed he went to Deming to ask him to do a seminar solely for the Navy.

Since Deming insisted that quality starts at the top, he was notorious for his refusal to deal initially with anyone below the top. "Where's your boss?" Deming demanded firmly. "Dr. Deming," Kirkpatrick replied just as firmly, "I am the boss." Deming laughed when he told the story on himself.

Kirkpatrick's quality program was getting no help from his superiors at the Pentagon in 1986 and '87. The navy assistant secretary in charge of the depots was a de-voted fan of competition, so he kept demanding more competition between depots that should have been coop-erating. A private management consulting firm working for the navy secretary released a critical study recom-mending a 15 percent personnel layoff and adoption of the same discredited quantity management principles that Kirkpatrick was trying to dump. Kirkpatrick had argued with the consultants about the need for a quality manage-ment approach, but in their final report, the civilian man-agement consultants had ignored him. Orders were obeyed, but the quality program stayed alive—quietly, to be sure, but alive.

In 1986, Colonel Jerald B. Gartman was assigned as commanding officer of the Naval Aviation Depot at Cherry Point, the only one of the six that is administered by the Marine Corps. Gartman, a Vietnam combat veteran, had been the production officer there from 1980 to '82, and he was remembered as being blunt, demanding, and when necessary, bad-tempered. Before he reported to take command, his new boss, Rear Admiral Kirkpatrick, told him to attend a four-day Deming seminar in Jacksonville, Florida. It worked.

When Gartman took command, he says, "I was truly trying to implement Dr. Deming's philosophy as I understood it." He now says that if he could do it over, he would do it differently because in 1986 he had "an imperfect understanding." He says he paid too much attention to measurements and techniques, and he now knows that "the human side is what really makes it work."

Howard, the former navy under secretary says, "They [Cherry Point] put together teams of people to look at these processes. They found that some of the individuals who were their troublemakers, who had been telling them that their system was all screwed up, were right. I recall one young man who was on the point of dismissal for being so obstinate and criticizing the process is now one of their most successful team leaders. It tells you that there are some advantages from a different approach."

If Gartman's understanding of the Deming philosophy was imperfect, it must have been pretty good nonetheless. "We were very successful," he admits. In 1988, Cherry Point won one of the first President's Awards for Quality—given by the Federal Quality Institute for "implementing quality management in an exemplary manner

. . . including the effective use of taxpayer dollars." * By practicing continual improvement, Cherry Point won again in 1993, the only repeat winner. The facility has increased its share of aircraft maintenance work from $249 million in 1988 to more than $400 million in 1993. (Depots try to get outside work from other government agencies, including the Army and Air Force, and from foreign governments that have bought used or refurbished American military aircraft. Aircraft repair is a highly competitive market.)

Quality in the Department of the Navy started with Broedling, Dockstader, Doherty, Kirkpatrick, Gartman, and a few others.† It did well, as they expected, but it was limited to a small part of the organization, and there was no guarantee it would continue. As the people who cared about quality management were transferred to new assignments, which was inevitable, what they had started could disappear. Originally, the problem of commanding-officer mobility had been raised as a possible barrier to adopting Deming's quality management system. Kirkpatrick rejected it on the basis that commanding officers may move from post to post, but they remain in the Navy or the Marine Corps. It was no different than an IBM executive transferring between divisions.

◆ ◆ ◆ ◆ ◆ ◆ ◆ ◆ ◆ ◆

* The President's Quality Award is modeled on the Malcolm Baldrige National Quality Award.

† William W. Scherkenbach, who was then head of the Deming program at the Ford Motor Company, is a 1968 graduate of the U.S. Naval Academy. He did his reserve service at the center in San Diego to help with the quality program.

As it turns out, mobility of naval personnel helps to spread total quality in the Department of the Navy.

Navy News Service told the story of Lieutenant Commander Chip Stilwell, an F-14 pilot assigned as production support officer on the aircraft carrier *Enterprise*. He had been taught Total Quality Leadership at Norfolk Naval Aviation Depot, where he'd seen the cost of reworking an F-14 cut by more than half. On the *Enterprise*, he said, he was getting "beat up every morning at the production meetings." His unit processed work permits in two trailers, widely separated, but it took nearly six days to get a work permit turned around, and nobody was happy. "I started thinking about it," Stilwell said, "and decided to apply some TQL to the situation."

By promising a 50 percent improvement, which no one believed, Stilwell got his two trailers moved together. He wrote a computer program to track work permits, and he started asking his personnel for suggestions on how to do the work better and quicker. The trailers were moved March 8. By the end of the month, production was up more than 56 percent and turnaround time was down from almost six days to not quite two days. In April, production improved more than 50 percent over March and turnaround time fell to not quite one day. In all, the productivity increase (the turnaround decrease) was 80 percent.

"The charts and graphs you're taught in TQL courses," Stilwell said, "are used to gauge your success and reinforce that what you're doing is right. But it's the people that matter. . . . All of our problems, and the solutions, were identified by blueshirts [sailors]." One of them was quoted as saying, "It was lousy here before Stilwell took over. We were all experiencing a lot of frustration and it killed our productivity." As an indication that morale in the unit is higher, the reenlistment rate is up.

So, mobility is proving to be no problem. Mobility certainly had nothing to do with the failure of the first quality improvement program that the Navy started with a vengeance in the early 1980s—quality circles. Within two years, all but a few had failed for the same reason they had failed in private industry—no one told the senior managers that they actually had to listen and respond to the suggestions made by the lesser ranks. As the Chip Stilwell story illustrates, that's not a problem in the quality approach now being used.

In the late 1980s, the quality enthusiasts got lucky. Some civilians appointed to high positions in the Department of the Navy came from private corporations where quality management systems were in place, and by 1988, Broedling, who had started it all in San Diego, was an adviser to the under secretary of the navy. Enough people who understood quality were in place so that when the budget was suddenly cut in 1989, causing an internal crisis, they could point to the quality approach as a financial solution. They had examples of money saved at aviation depots and at shipyards, which had also used a quality management approach. When Dan Howard, a career foreign service officer, was named under secretary of the navy in 1990, he was asked to lead the quality management effort.

In a paper written in 1993 to explain why quality is working in the department, Howard and two colleagues said that quality management can't work unless leaders "recognize a crisis and experience a jointly felt need for change." In 1989, everyone recognized the crisis and the need for change. All the Navy and the Marine Corps could see in the future were budget cuts, base closings, and reductions in personnel. A number of people in the military services have observed since then that if private corporations faced in 1989 what the services faced, the corporations would have had no choice but to declare bankruptcy and close.

The Department of the Navy is a huge business. The seven naval shipyards by themselves employ 75,000 people and spend $4 billion. "That puts [the shipyards] right after Coca-Cola and just ahead of Inland Steel on the *Fortune* 500," Howard says. "We have about a million people in the Navy, in the Marine Corps, and in our civilian organizations," he adds. "The budget is coming down very quickly, but we're still spending $92 billion of taxpayers' money this year [1992]." The question becomes, how do you get an organization that gigantic to change? For Howard, the answer is consensus.

In a September 1992 conversation with Deming, whose four-day seminar he had taken, Howard told him, "One of the things you didn't tell me about in great detail was the importance of building a consensus." To Howard, that does not mean that everyone enthusiastically agrees, claps their hands, and jumps on board. "It means," he says, "that you can have a direction, an idea, a policy, a decision in which everyone can agree *enough* that they don't destroy it, that they don't torpedo it, that they don't stab it in the back."

Many Americans who praise the consensus management system in Japan don't understand that Japanese consensus means exactly what Howard describes. As an example, when a policy has been debated and accepted in a Japanese corporation, it is written and circulated to those executives who took part in the debate. Each puts his personal chop—his or (very rarely) her name seal—at the end of the report. Occasionally, one of the chops will be sideways. That person is announcing to his colleagues, "I disagree, but I will do or say nothing contrary." We believe that it would be helpful if American executives had some similar way to officially and quietly register their disapproval within the group, but publicly join the consensus.

In the old department, there was no consensus. Linda Doherty says the people in charge of aviation, surface ships, and submarines "were in very strong competition for funding. . . . Those people got evaluated on what portion of the budget they were able to command and commandeer through Congress." That had a predictable result. "The real nefarious warfare going on before you got to the other services," she says, "was within the Navy itself for pots of money." That ended with the Department of the Navy Review Commission, twenty-five of the most senior people, military and civilian, in the Navy and the Marine Corps, put together by Howard. They met five hours a day, five days a week for months in 1992 in what was described as "a long and painful consensus-building process." In the end, the commission saved $12 billion and produced what the Department of Defense calls "the most well-balanced long-range plan in the department" and did it during what Howard has described as the most difficult budget period since 1946, and perhaps since 1918.

"Consensus building," Howard says, "is very hard; it's painstaking." In the Navy and the Marine Corps, Howard is dealing with career professionals, highly successful men and women with deeply held beliefs on what is right and what is wrong. "You first have to convince people who think that they're already doing a very good job," Howard says, "that there is a better way, that they can change, that they should change, that there's an advantage to changing." Howard explains that traditionally in the Department of the Navy when there was a budget crunch, senior commanders would hang on to the hardware—ships and planes—and the people to staff them, and they'd save money by cutting education, reducing training, letting bases and buildings deteriorate, and leaving sailors at sea longer. The inevitable result was some unhappy military personnel leaving the service.

This budget cut is different. The department since World War II has existed to win a war against the Soviet Union. With that threat gone, the Department of the Navy is being forced to go back to Deming's 14 Points and redefine its purpose—what does it do, and why does it do it? "We are trying to refocus," Howard says, "I think with some success, on the role for the Navy and the Marine Corps in the twenty-first century." Since the senior officers now understand that the Navy Department is a system, they are writing strategic goals with that in mind. "We're actually taking money out of buying bullets in some areas," Howard says, "and putting it into things like rehabilitation of family housing or of bachelor enlisted quarters because we understand that that's part of the equation as well, that we're a total system. . . . No one can remember any time in the history of this country when we have decreased the defense budget and increased the money that we're spending on our people, on their housing, on their education, on their pay."

To adopt the Deming quality management system in the Department of the Navy has occasionally required some fancy footwork. The Deming method, for instance, is opposed to personnel rankings, but federal law requires annual personal performance appraisals.

There were about 2,300 employees at the Naval Aviation Supply Office in Philadelphia in 1988, according to the department's total quality newsletter. The agency controlled an inventory worth $15 billion and was the supplier to the six aviation repair depots. The people at Philadelphia were trying to adopt a quality system and found that the performance appraisals got in the way. The appraisals, for one thing, determined how performance bonus money was awarded. The law, therefore, required competition where cooperation was essential. The law in this case may have been "a ass, a idiot," as Charles Dickens wrote, but it had to be obeyed anyway.

To satisfy the law and adopt a quality system, the managers in Philadelphia voted to be ranked as a team in areas such as customer satisfaction and continual improvement. A similar effort was made with employees, and a team was established to recommend a recognition program. The team took the performance bonus money and turned it into "special act" awards for teams of employees who contributed to quality goals. Margaret Shetz, director of employee relations, said, "They preferred a system where everyone worked toward the same goals and where everyone shared equally in the bonus money." Under the old performance appraisal, about 25 percent of the employees got 90 percent of the money. Under the new system, according to Shetz, "99 percent of our employees share all the award money."

There's more to it. The award team came up with two other nonmonetary recognition systems. One allows individuals to recognize other individuals and thank them for their help. The other is a group-to-group award, given twice a year on Recognition Days in the spring and fall. Shetz said "employees have consistently approved what we're doing with the appraisals and awards money. People get a real kick out of getting a "You Made a Difference' award from coworkers, and they like to give them as well."

Howard says that one of the things the Navy Department has learned in recent wars, hot and cold, and in the quality system is the importance of people. "We have the finest group of people in uniform in the Navy and the Marine Corps that we've ever had in this country's history," he says. "I've seen our civilian employees at work as well, and I violently disagree with the view . . . that the people who work in government are lazy, because they're not. But most of them are being strangled to death by the system."

Doherty says people have to be coaxed out of the old system and into the quality system. "You can only do that when you treat everybody in a way that helps them to make their contributions," she says. "You have to understand their individual differences, and you have to give them what they need so that they can perform and do better. In the Department of the Navy that's much more important than just doing a job. We ask young men and young women to put their lives on the line."

Change is taking place in the Navy and Marine Corps, but it is taking time, and that is one of the complaints. Patrick Townsend, a quality consultant and a retired Marine major with twenty years' experience, says the quality system being installed is far too slow and much too elite. He says there is too much top down and not enough bottom up, so that the people who have to deal with day-to-day problems have the least say now in what is being changed. His criticism is of *how* quality is being achieved, not with the quality approach itself. Even at that, it is difficult to argue with the success of the department's approach.

Balboa Naval Hospital in San Diego uses process action teams to track down, study, and solve specific problems. One team increased the number of patients discharged on time from 50 percent to 73 percent. Another team decreased unnecessary time in the hospital for new mothers and infants by 70 percent. Another cut the number of patients who had to be sent to a non-Navy hospital because of a shortage of beds at Balboa from eight to ten a month to two or three a month. That saved $250,000 annually. It was all done under the Department of the Navy quality approach. (Incidentally, the word "approach" is used because any "program" in the Navy and the Marine Corps has a specific end; the quality approach does not. Similarly, Ronald D. Schmidt at Zytec argues against use of the word *program*. "It [quality] is not a program," he says; "it is a way of life!")

A process action team at a supply office studied how stock numbers were assigned, eliminated several steps and supervisory checks, and cut processing time from 138 days to 35 days. The team cut the backlog in one area by 68 percent.

Even if the quality approach had not started, the Navy and the Marine Corps would be changing anyway. The budget crisis would still exist. A new mission statement would still have to be written. The revolution in communications would still have to be dealt with. All the military services are organized as hierarchical structures, the same top-down, boss-to-underlings model that is generally described in Exodus and was used by Moses to lead the Israelites out of Egypt. A naval officer on active duty recently wondered out loud how long that venerable chain of command could be strictly maintained when the lowest seaman in the service can anonymously send a fax to the chief of naval operations. Quality system or no quality system, the Department of the Navy could not have stayed the same. "Our leadership clearly understood," Howard says, "that if we didn't create our own future, somebody else was going to create it for us."

"Every system in the world grows barnacles," Howard says. "You have a process which is pristine, which is perfect. As time goes along, someone makes a mistake, or something happens in the marketplace, and so you create another step in the process to account for it, to make sure that no one can make that particular mistake again. . . . As time goes along, you add another step and another step, and before long, you have a system that responds to all of those previous inputs, but it has become so cumbersome that it's almost impossible to get things done. That exists in the private sector in this country; it exists tenfold in government."

The Navy is scraping off the barnacles, changing, shifting its focus, becoming a smaller, better-managed, less expensive force. Doing that has not been pleasant. Facilities are closing, people in uniform and out are being let go, whole units are disappearing, being decommissioned. "You have no idea how painful that is," Howard says. "Everyone understands how painful a layoff is. That's what we're doing; we're laying people off, but it's a permanent layoff. We're closing the plant; we're selling off the real estate." He says some of the units that are disappearing have existed for fifty to a hundred years, and some of the facilities go back to "the birth of the nation." Without the quality approach, what has been painful may well have been all but unbearable.

Howard says that the Deming quality management system has made it possible for senior Navy officials to make tough decisions that they did not want to make. "If we didn't have the degree of certainty in our own minds about what is important to the future of this country," he says, "why it's important for them to have this kind of Navy and Marine Corps, I don't think we would have the guts to make the decisions that we're making. . . . Without profound knowledge, we would not be where we are!"

◆ ◆ ◆ ◆ ◆

When Rear Admiral John Kirkpatrick and others were first discussing the quality program, they called it Total Quality Control, a name often used in Japan. Kirkpatrick didn't like that because "control" has specific meanings in the armed forces, and "quality" isn't one of them. At one of the early meetings, he asked for another name, and a behavioral psychologist named Nancy Warren suggested Total Quality Management, since it seemed to her that management was key. Kirkpatrick liked it, as did, it seems, most quality consultants on earth no matter what they teach. TQM was born.

Admiral Frank Kelso took over as chief of naval operations in June 1990. He endorsed the Total Quality Management approach, but not the name. It seemed to him to have more to do with leadership than with management, hence, the current name in the Department of the Navy, Total Quality Leadership. By whatever name, it is the Deming quality management system, and there is reason to hope that it will spread in the United States government.

As we've mentioned, President Clinton knows about quality management systems in government, and at least four members of the Cabinet—Donna Shalala, Hazel O'Leary, Mike Espy, and Robert Reich—are acquainted with or have used quality management systems. Laurie Broedling, who left her Navy job to carry quality to the Defense Department and NASA, was a member of Vice President Al Gore's task force on reinventing government, officially the National Performance Review. When its final report was issued, she went back to NASA and Defense.

As for the others who played prominent parts in the Navy TQL effort, Steve Dockstader still works with NPRDC in San Diego, and Linda Doherty is director of the TQL office for the Department of the Navy in Washington. Dan Howard has retired from the foreign service and will join Unisys in Japan, where he was stationed years ago. John Kirkpatrick retired from the Navy and is now with the Process Management Institute, a quality consulting firm in Minneapolis headed by Lou Schultz. Schultz, by the way, is a longtime friend of Ronald D. Schmidt and helped with the transformation of Zytec. Small world, indeed. Jerald B. Gartman retired from the Marine Corps and is now a quality consultant in North Carolina. He says about half his work is with the military, half with private industry.

◆ ◆ ◆ ◆ ◆

The highly successful effort to introduce the Deming quality management system in the Department of the Navy is one of the military's better kept secrets. A computer search of three national newspapers turned up only two articles printed between 1990 and 1993 about the department's effort. Both were in *USA Today*. The *New York Times* had no article, but did print a letter in April 1992 from Dan Howard, then under secretary of the navy, answering a critic of government and saying that the Department of the Navy had adopted a quality management system. "We are committed to a continuous process of improvement," Howard wrote, "to breaking down the conditions that make for a hidebound, inefficient bureaucracy." If anything at all has appeared in the *Wall Street Journal* in more than three years, the computer search did not find it.

That illustrates one of the problems in trying to get the public involved in the debate about the economic future of the United States: The people who normally lead national debates—the politicians and the press—don't yet understand what ought to be debated. That could change.

The bellwether of journalism is the *New York Times*. It is the accepted newspaper of record in the United States and one of the more influential newspapers in the English-speaking world. The publisher, Arthur Sulzberger, Jr., told a reporter, "We produce the finest newspaper certainly in this country, and probably in the world." Its circulation is about 1.2 million, well below the 2 million circulation of *USA Today* and the *Wall Street Journal*. But the *Times* has influence beyond its numbers, especially among national politicians and other journalists. Members of Congress sometimes quote the *Times* when calling for investigations or committee hearings, and other journalists sometimes treat it with troublesome reverence. A television correspondent in France in the early 1970s called his network foreign desk in New York suggesting a story about pollution in the Mediterranean that could close beaches and severely damage tourism around Nice and St. Tropez, weakening the French economy. The foreign editor in New York agreed that it was a good story, but turned it down because, "We haven't seen anything like that in the *Times.*"

With that sort of influence, the odds are that if the paper became interested in quality management, other news organizations would become interested as well. That is why the national debate may change. The *Times* is not only interested, it is in the process of adopting the Deming quality management system with considerable success, but not without some pain.*

The *Times* has been losing advertising because of the failure of other businesses—principally New York City department stores—that were heavy newspaper ad users. There is no danger of the paper closing, but if a way could be found to improve the paper and reduce costs, so much the better. The *Times* is not only a business, it is a family enterprise and has been since Adolph Ochs bought the paper in 1896. Only family members have been publishers since then, and the *Times* is a matter of family pride.

Late in 1989, Lance R. Primis, then president of the *New York Times*, arranged to meet Dr. Deming to talk about quality. More meetings were planned, and Deming asked Dr. Joyce Orsini to help with the project. Orsini is a student of Deming's and a quality consultant. She is also director of the Deming Scholars M.B.A. program and as-

♦ ♦ ♦ ♦ ♦ ♦ ♦ ♦ ♦ ♦

* For a report on the often personal upset caused by changing to the Deming quality management system, see Ken Auletta's article "Opening Up the Times" in the June 28, 1993, issue of the *New Yorker*.

sociate professor of management systems at Fordham University in the Bronx, New York City. The three of them—Primis, Deming, and Orsini—met several times in late 1989 to talk about a quality management system and how it might work at the *Times*.

Deming suggested that *Times* senior officers attend his four-day seminar in Washington, D.C., in late January 1990. Primis went, along with Sulzberger, then deputy publisher; Russell T. Lewis, then executive vice president; and John M. O'Brien, deputy general manager. Then for four months, every Monday morning, Primis, Sulzberger (who would become publisher in January 1992), and the senior staff met with Orsini to discuss how best to incorporate the Deming quality management system into the *New York Times*, which is a bit more difficult than it sounds.

As Orsini learned when she started meeting with *Times* executives, the newspaper has two different sets of customers, and what would satisfy, please, or delight each group is not necessarily the same thing, and in a few cases, what will please one will infuriate the other. In reality, a newspaper is two separate businesses existing in an always uneasy, but essential, symbiotic relationship.

For one set of customers, the paper's product—what is being delivered—is news. That customer is the reader, and to please the customer-reader, the news must be complete, unbiased, and understandable. The more you meet or exceed readers' expectations, the more readers you will attract. (That is not strictly true, but it's the only sensible way to run a paper.) The more readers you get, the more you will delight the other set of customers, the advertisers.

To the customer-advertiser, the paper's product—

what is being delivered—is the customer-readers. The advertisers are not principally concerned with the news but with how many people are reading it and will, therefore, see the advertisements printed beside the columns of news.

Both sets of customers are concerned with the newspaper's reputation. For example, a reader of, or an advertiser in, the *Times* is highly unlikely to buy, in either sense, a supermarket tabloid.

(To add another element, one reason readers buy a particular paper is for the advertising, to see who's got what on sale, or what's in fashion, or what people are buying. If you go into a medium-sized city and want to know how the economy there is doing, you can read the ads in the local paper and make an incredibly good guess. If there are no ads for new car dealers, but the classified ads are filled with used cars for sale, don't plan on opening a designer boutique. If liquor stores are advertising premium brands and the carpet store has an ad that is *not* about a sale, you are in Boomtown.)

In newspaper parlance, the people committed to satisfying the customer-reader are "editorial." The people committed to pleasing the customer-advertiser are "business." In the normal course of events, business sells advertising, editorial reports news. It would seem to be a functional, cooperative, and sensible arrangement, and it usually is. Each leaves the other alone. Usually. Not always. Not in any medium.

In 1970, a network documentary, produced by the editorial side, refused to alter the disgusting, even horrifying film showing a migrant farm labor camp, newly owned through acquisition by one of the network's larger advertisers, one that was important to the business side. In the last quarter of 1970, that advertiser had bought $2 million dollars' worth of ads on the network. In the first quarter of 1971, after the documentary, it bought no ads on that network, but millions of dollars' worth on the other two television networks.

Now you know why the business side sometimes goes into gastric distress at what the editorial side does: What is best for the customer-reader is sometimes what is worst for the customer-advertiser, and the network or newspaper business suffers.

However, if the editorial side begins to shape the news to please the advertiser, the paper will lose the respect of the reader, who will stop buying it. As the paper loses readers, it will become less attractive to advertisers, and those advertisers will eventually stop buying space in the paper. Without the advertising, the paper cannot continue; no major newspaper in the United States can exist solely on the money it earns from readers' subscriptions and newsstand sales. No matter how you approach the newspaper business, you cannot have one set of customers without the other set of customers, and their needs can be diametrically opposed. Over the years, to protect one set from the other, a wall has gone up between editorial and business that makes the Great Wall of China look like a line drawn in the dirt. At the old Time-Life Corporation in the days of founder Henry Luce, the editorial-business separation was referred to as "church and state" and was treated with near-constitutional reverence.

Now, does anyone remember point 9 of Deming's 14 Points? Break down barriers between staff areas.

"There is some contact between business and editorial," Orsini writes, "[but] still not much." At the *Times*, there are now several committees dealing with issues in all departments, including improved internal communications. Hundreds of teams dealing with specifics are working in all areas of the newspaper. Editorial and business sometimes serve together on committees and teams, and at more senior levels, business and editorial apparently are more available to each other, and, Orsini adds, "Everyone sees progress."

There is notable progress in other areas as well.

There is a third business at a newspaper without which the first two businesses wouldn't have a chance. Editorial can produce prizewinning articles and businesses can sell the advertising to pay for them, and neither activity means a thing until production prints the newspaper.

The *Times* opened up a new printing plant in Edison, New Jersey, on September 22, 1992, and it went into full production in the spring of 1993. The first color was printed in the *New York Times Book Review* in June. All production department managers have been given statistical process control training, and the plant is managed with the Deming quality system. There is already one noticeable benefit for readers.

The *Times*, like other newspapers, has always bought printer's ink from several suppliers for the same reason businesses traditionally use several suppliers—to get the best possible price. As we've mentioned before, however, the best price in the long run may not be the cheapest purchase price, especially in the newspaper business where readers are irritated by cheap ink that rubs off on their fingers as they read the paper. In 1991, the *Times* adopted point 5 of the 14 Points and chose a single ink supplier on the condition that the paper and supplier work cooperatively to develop a better-quality ink. They did, and the new ink reduces reader rub-off about 60 percent. They're still working cooperatively to improve the ink even more. By the way, the cost of the better-quality ink remains competitive.

Orsini continues to meet with *Times* officials, committees, and groups, and there is good reason to believe that the Deming management system is spreading to the newspaper's parent, the New York Times Company, which acquired the *Boston Globe* in 1993. It already owned thirty-one other newspapers, five television stations, two radio stations, twenty magazines, and other companies. Primis, who was president of the newspaper, moved up to become president of the parent company. (Russell Lewis took over at the paper.) Orsini held a luncheon seminar for company officials in May, and early in August 1993, at least four company officers were at a four-day Deming seminar in San Diego. With the *Times* and other Times Company papers involved, perhaps the press will begin to lead the national debate on the future of the United States.

10

$\bullet \quad \bullet \quad \bullet \quad \bullet \quad \bullet$

Governments

There can be no conflict between good economics
and good morals.
—*Henry Ford*

In 1843, Henry L. Ellsworth, first commissioner of the
U.S. Patent Office, suggested that his agency would soon
close because there was nothing left to invent.
"Advancement of the arts from year to year," he wrote
with his quill pen in his candlelit office, "taxes our
credulity and seems to presage the arrival of that period
when human improvement must end." The proposal does
not seem to have caused any excitement in the administration of John Tyler, and the office remained open. It still
is. In 1992, it granted 109,728 patents, about 435 every
working day.

Ellsworth's suggestion is remembered as nothing more
than a historical curiosity, something that people can
laugh at on two levels—his arrogance to think that he
could predict when "human improvement must end" and
his utter folly in believing that government would get
smaller. According to the Institute for Policy Innovation,
in 1992 for the first time, more civilians worked in federal, state, and local governments than worked in private
manufacturing. That was partly because fewer people
worked in manufacturing, but the rate of growth in gov-

ernment employment would have guaranteed the same result one day.

Manufacturing creates wealth; government disposes of wealth. When you have more people spending it than you have making it, the odds are that you have a problem. It is an even bigger problem when the people who order the spending at the federal level—basically, the Congress and the president—know that spending ever-larger amounts of money is the only way they can appear to provide service to the voters. State and local spending is smaller, but often no wiser.

In constant 1990 dollars, governments spent about $23,000 per household in 1992, nearly double what was spent in 1960. There are a greater number of households now, so the spending is up even more than it first appears. As a percentage of the total economy—the gross domestic product—spending by governments amounted to about 26 percent in 1960 and 37 percent now—from about a quarter to more than a third.

Governments, as a rule, do not spend money unless there is a public demand to spend it—better schools, universal health care, better highways, safer streets. What actually happens is that the people demand better quality, but the federal, state, and local governments are not organized to produce quality. As a result, governments spend every penny they raise or borrow to persuade voters that those in office are doing all that they can to take care of the citizen-consumer: "We're gonna whip this thing 'cause we're spending seventy-two gigabillion bucks!" Since governments cannot create wealth, the bucks they spend must be raised either in taxes, hurting us, or in borrowing, hurting our children. Either way, there will never be enough money. As newspaper columnist Tom Wicker noted in 1968, "Government expands to absorb revenues and then some."

In the 1970s, John Stewart was an executive director of the National Commission on Productivity. He is now a director of McKinsey & Company, the management consultants, and remains concerned with the economy. He says the federal government correctly *identified* slipping productivity as the problem, but "has not *understood* the problem, not articulated the issue well, nor pointed out the solutions. Government is still driven by the budget, which is antithetical to the new quality philosophy."

What the Deming management system says, in effect, is that you can save money by concentrating on the system and organizing and improving that system to produce quality. You cannot save money by concentrating on the budget. Instead of deciding what you want to accomplish—your aim—you are deciding what you want to spend. In effect, you are inspecting the budget. You are dealing with the result rather than with the system that produces the result. If you want to save money, you must study the processes of government and transform the system to produce the results that you want for less money. For a government or a business, saving money requires a long-term view, and Stewart says officials in Washington are concerned not with long-term efficiency but with how much political good they can get from every dollar spent. "Continuous improvement is not rewarded," he says. "Continuous budget expansion is."

In the summer of 1993, there was a great deal of talk in Washington about "cutting the budget." Cutting the budget in a business or a family means that you have less money to spend. Expenses must come down. That is what cutting a budget means. That is *not* what cutting the budget means with the federal government, because the federal government plays accounting tricks that many people don't understand, which is probably just as well. If people and companies tried to do this, the results would range from financial chaos to criminal charges.

When a federal official speaks of cutting the budget, he does not mean there will be less money to spend. He means there will be less of an *increase*, but there *will* be an increase. To any other human on the face of the earth, spending more money means a budget increase; to the federal government, spending more money, but not as *much* more as it might have spent, is a budget cut.

It works this way: The budget debate does not start with how much was spent last year. It starts with how much will be spent this year if the government continues to do what it did—that is, last year's budget plus money for inflation, for the increase in population, and for a couple of "fudge factors," which are usually pretty fat so that the "budget cuts" to come will look better. Hence, a budget cut is only cutting the increase (except for the Department of Defense since 1989). It is dishonest and misleading, and it is not going to change, because it helps keep elected officials in office by letting them brag about "cutting the budget."

Federal officials have created that problem for themselves; many others are built into the system.

Stewart says most of the federal government, including the legislative and executive branches, has no concept of a team approach or consensus, no long-term purpose, and few seem to understand the investment trade-offs that are needed for our future. "So in a sense," he concludes, "our collective economy—the government, the

Congress, the executive, the corporations—reflect the same disarray that existed ten years ago inside the auto and other industries that had not figured out the new quality philosophy." The new quality philosophy appears to have paid off for those American companies that have figured it out. The news magazine *Far Eastern Economic Review* found in a survey of its Asian subscribers that Germany was rated first in quality products. Japan had slipped to second, and the United States had almost caught up, only .02 percent behind Japan. Quality progress is being made in industry, but there seems to be much less progress in service, including governments.

For most of the history of the United States, the federal government played such a small part in the daily lives of most citizens that what it did or didn't do was far less important than it is now. It is only since World War II that the American people have turned to government to solve every conceivable social and economic problem and to solve them, of course, without raising taxes—guaranteeing a double disappointment. Taxes have been raised; problems have not been solved. Peter Drucker writes, "None of the U.S. programs of the last forty years in which we tried to tackle a social problem through government action has produced significant results."

The same statement could be made of economic problems and government action. It is only since World War II that trade and commerce have become global rather than national and that the need for brains in industry has far outstripped the need for brawn. In the past fifty years, the changes in the social and economic lives of Americans have been enormous, but the attitude and the organization of the federal government are all but unchanged.

"The government should understand," Stewart says, "how its own actions are contrary to the success of the American economy in the international world."

To change what goes on throughout the federal government, officials must understand that government is a system, and any system, even the government system, can be organized to produce quality. That can be done exactly as it has been done in Zytec, Westinghouse Technical and Vocational High School, the Hospital Corporation of America, the Department of the Navy, and the *New York Times*, to name only those in this book. We have not yet mentioned Community Quality Councils, which are spreading across the country. They are local cooperative groups of business, labor, government, and education that work on local problems in all those areas.

In Kingsport, Tennessee, a council helped the Kingsport Foundry improve its system and win orders that would have gone to Taiwan. The foundry had been going broke; it is now expanding. In Erie, Pennsylvania, a council saved the county government money in its prison system, reduced the family service agency's waiting list from seventy-seven to seventeen, decreased the police department's emergency response time, helped the college improve its academic advisory system, helped the high school district start a course in the fundamentals of quality, and showed a local manufacturer how to produce a product in three days instead of thirty. The Erie Community Quality Council spent no money to do all of that. Its motto is "No money, no politics, no hidden agenda."

Which means that the federal government will never adopt that system.

But it could adopt the Deming quality management system. All that is required to start is for senior government officials to answer the first questions: What are we doing? Why are we doing it? What is the aim of government? What are its mission, values, and guiding principles? It is almost frightening to imagine what the answers would be now, assuming that they were honest answers and not the usual Pecksniffian puffery that often passes for honest debate in Washington.

Which gets us to a problem or perhaps to a solution; we can't be certain yet. "Quality, like ethics, cannot be delegated," Dr. Deming said repeatedly. In May 1960, the White House under President Dwight David Eisenhower insisted in public and at the United Nations that a U-2 spy plane shot down over the Soviet Union was nothing but an innocent weather plane. That seemed to mark, at least in the twentieth century, the beginning of a continuing slide in ethical behavior in official Washington. Many American voters now routinely accept that campaign promises by candidates have no meaning, and the candidates, once elected, routinely ignore what they have promised without apparent regret or even a hint of remorse.

In effect, members of government are using the popular quantity technique of management by objective, doing whatever is necessary to gain their objective—remaining in office. Therefore, the perceived definition of ethics in government becomes "whatever keeps me in office," and too often that sort of goal-oriented behavior leads, as Dr. Brian Joiner suggests, from unethical to immoral to illegal behavior—without the person involved understanding what is happening. The unethical and illogical become normal. In 1977, four years after he resigned from the presidency to escape impeachment for Watergate, former President Richard M. Nixon told David Frost in a May 19 television interview, "When the President does it, that means that it is not illegal." The comment is so patently absurd that it was cited in the 1980 edition of *Bartlett's Familiar Quotations.*

We have never found a quality company (school, hospital) that was not also an ethical company. We do not know precisely which comes first or how they are related; indeed, there is no proof that they *are* related, and if they are, we do not know what the relationship is. All we can report with accuracy is that ethics and quality appear to coexist. We *hope* they are related, and we *hope* the relationship is that quality leads to ethics. For instance, it is possible to imagine an ethical company that has not yet become a quality company. On the other hand, it is not possible to imagine a quality company that is not yet an ethical company. If that is the relationship—if quality breeds ethics—then the adoption of a quality management system in the federal government should lead to a more ethical government and restore faith in our elected leaders.

Americans have been driven to such cynicism that fewer than 15 percent of the people said in the summer of 1993 that "they trust the U.S. government to do what is right most of the time." If more people knew what Congress and the president meant when they talked about "cutting the budget," the number might be even lower. Even at 15 percent, however, it is the lowest it has been since the poll's results were first published in 1964, when more than 60 percent of the people trusted government. If quality leads to ethics and the government adopts a quality system, then the American people's trust in government could be restored.

If our guess is wrong, and the true relationship is that

government must have ethics to achieve quality, then—well, perhaps it's better not to consider that possibility. In some cases, even reporters prefer optimism, particularly when the alternative is not simple pessimism but utter despair.

Whatever the United States government decides to do about a quality management system, it will take time, especially to unlearn those things that members of government believe—as do most of the rest of the American people, for that matter. Just as then President George Bush believed that "competition never hurt anything," Vice President Al Gore believes the same thing, and he heads the National Performance Review. At a meeting in June 1993 in Philadelphia to listen to ideas for improvement of government, the vice president interrupted a speaker to argue that cooperation did not motivate people, competition did.*

Even those who think in-house competition (conflict) is wonderful will admit that it causes job stress, which they often defend as "creative." If the International Labor Organization is correct, it is much more costly than it is creative. The U.N. agency says job stress now costs American business and industry $200 billion a year, and it may cost Great Britain about 10 percent of its total economy. Other studies in Canada, France, Japan, and Sweden reached similar conclusions. The costs come from absenteeism, health care, and worker compensation claims. In California, according to a news report, "a state judge collected [worker compensation] money after claiming he suffered a stroke as a result of being overworked by the

• • • • • • • • • •

* I was the speaker. (C.C.-M.)

increased caseload of worker compensation claims." The ILO's expert on job stress was quoted as saying, "We think the answer is in work organization and management style." He suggested worker participation and labor-management teamwork, both of which are part of the Deming quality management system.

It is easy to understand why levels of stress are going up. Our lives are changing and our institutions seem inadequate to help us cope with that change.

Americans started as farmers. Each of us knew exactly where he or she fit in the family and society, precisely what had to be done when. Children grew up knowing what work was; they saw their parents, often their grandparents as well, work every day. As the children got older, they had their own chores, and they learned that if you want to eat, you work. For farm families and the societies in which they lived, farm work came first; everything else came later. (Public schools are still scheduled to meet agricultural needs, letting out in the summer, the growing season, so the students can help their families in the fields. There's been no massive need for that for sixty years or more.)

Mills and mill towns came next and were somewhat more difficult to understand, but were still relatively straightforward. The system was fairly obvious, and anyone in town knew that raw materials went in one end of the factory, workers and machines did things to the materials, and finished goods came out the other end. Kids could no longer watch both their parents work, but at least they could see the mill where one worked. In the typical family, the husband went to work at the mill and the woman worked at home. Americans like to pretend that's still the typical family, but it isn't.

In the modern economy, huge corporations have plants and offices around the world. Understanding the system is often difficult because the employee may have grown up across the country or even in another country. What is being made may not have existed until five or ten years ago and may cease to exist in five or ten more years. That factory may not make the whole thing, just a part of it, so no one knows what his or her work accomplishes. If the company is successful, it may be acquired by some larger company, or bought out, or broken up and sold off. If the company is less successful, it may be acquired by some larger company, or bought out, or broken up and sold off, or go bankrupt.

Children not only may not see their parents work; they may not see their parents during the work day at all. More American children than ever before—about 25 percent—live with only one parent, and that figure is going up. Where there are two parents, both of them often have to work outside the home to make ends meet. By 1992, nearly 58 percent of women sixteen or older were in the labor force, compared with about 38 percent in 1963. About 22 million mothers with children—about 63 percent—now work full time, nearly three times as many as did so thirty years ago.

The agricultural society and the mill towns are gone. A quality management system will not magically make new systems or new technologies go away. However, quality management will make it easier to cope, to understand what is happening and reduce the confusion, anxiety, and frustration that seem so much a part of everyday life. If nothing else, with a quality management system, everyone inside that system knows precisely where he or she fits and what he or she must do. People who work in quality systems not only say they are happier at work; they say they are happier at home as well. Other management systems have not been able to deal with the pressures of modern work and home life because they are not complete. They may have had some elements of quality management, but some elements are not enough. You need all of them. To illustrate that point in a paper on quality in education, Dr. Myron Tribus isolated the elements in quality management and identified them as philosophy, vision, strategy, skills, resources, rewards, and organization. He studied what would happen if any one of those elements was missing from a system and drew this simple figure to illustrate the loss.

The only line where there might be a mild quibble is the last where all the elements are present, and it is labeled "Success!" In all probability, that is true; certainly, that's the way to bet because the odds are enormously in your favor. However, success is not inevitable. Think back to Profound Knowledge and the theory of variation. It says there is variation in all things—*all* things. "You could make a list of companies," Deming said, "doing famously well and violating all the good rules of management, applying the worst kind of management that you could imagine, yet they're doing well. They're fortunate, plain lucky in having a product that wins no matter what." There are other companies trying to use the Deming management system "and not doing very well," he explained. "But think how they would be with *worse* management." A company doing well with bad management could do so much better with good management, and a company doing poorly with good management, would be so much worse without it. William Scherkenbach remembers, "Dr. Deming says, 'Don't confuse suc-

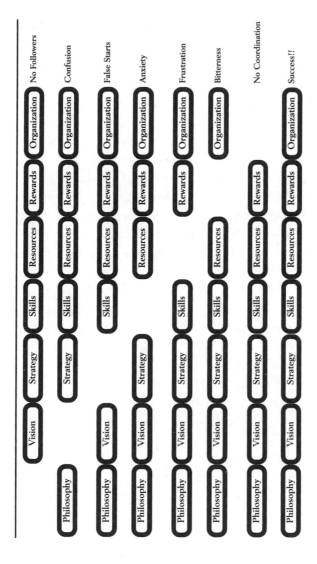

ESSENTIAL LINKS IN THE CHAIN OF SUCCESS. If one link is missing, the chain will fail.

Figure 4. This diagram was drawn for us by Myron Tribus, who says he adapted it from a presentation by Dr. Clara Jean Ersoz, who in turn says she got it from someone but doesn't remember who. We are grateful to all of them.

cess with success.' You've got to ask yourself, 'How much better could it be?' "

Sometimes a company does worse while trying to do better. The Wallace Company that filed for bankruptcy fifteen months after it won the Baldrige Award is one example, but not the only one.

A major American corporation, which we won't name—our aim is to help, not hurt—wanted to win the Malcolm Baldrige National Quality Award in 1994. Baldrige criteria became the basis for an internal competition between divisions to get ready for the company-wide application. It quickly became obvious that doing one's bit toward winning the award was one of the requirements for promotions and pay raises. Different divisions began to hire Baldrige examiners as consultants; some even hired professional writers to handle the applications, but that wasn't enough. The Baldrige criteria are written with the legal precision that a graded contest requires, but legal precision does not breed language clarity, so translators had to be hired to tell the writers what each of the "areas to be addressed" meant. A person who was involved says, "Quality became an essay contest, a liberal arts subject."

It gets worse.

If you are going to have an internal competition, you must have internal examiners, and if they are to use the Baldrige criteria, they must be trained to understand those criteria. In the Malcolm Baldrige National Quality Award itself, examiners are men and women who are acquainted with quality systems and have a deep understanding of statistics and measurement. Even with that advanced background, they are trained for four days on how to judge before they go to a contestant company. At the company that wanted the award in 1994, the internal examiners were less well qualified, but four days of Baldrige training was deemed to be too much, so it was cut to two days, and later to one.

Category Four of the Baldrige criteria asks about employee training and education, so a corporate executive ordered two days of training for all employees to help satisfy the requirement. As bad fortune would have it, the only two-day training course then in place was—you guessed it!—the one for examiners. It hadn't been cut to one day yet. Men and women from the factory floor took the two-day course and returned to the factory floor inadequately trained as Baldrige examiners, a skill that is in limited demand and likely will not improve their lives. However, it may stretch their imaginations while they try to puzzle out what in hell the company was thinking of.

It goes on, but there's no purpose in any more detail. The company eventually gave up its goal of the Baldrige in 1994. Company officials may or may not be any wiser, but they are definitely poorer. There are no firm figures available, but the best guess is that the company spent at least $100 million and, if training and employee-time costs are added, perhaps as much as $500 million to accomplish nothing of value.

Setting out to win the Baldrige Award is the same as government setting out to cut the budget. Each is the wrong goal. You must set out to achieve a better product or service at less cost for the delight of the customers or the citizens by using a quality management system. If you do that, your company may well win the Baldrige, and the company or the government certainly will save money. This isn't quantum mechanics, folks; we're talking carts and horses and the proper order thereof.

However, change is difficult even when making things better, as Samuel Johnson observed, and that is true this time as well. The potential difficulty is easiest to see in health care, which has been one of the largest and most consistent areas of job creation for several years. About 10 million people now work in the field. If health care adopted the quality management system, it is all but certain that some of those people, perhaps a lot of those people, would be out of work. As it stands today, about 25 percent of hospital workers deal with insurance forms, bills, and debt collection. A quality management system would streamline financial matters, and most of the people in the hospitals, the insurance agencies, and government at all levels who handle money matters would not be needed. The loss of those jobs could be a terrible problem.

If we do not adopt a quality management system, the problem will be much worse.

By no stretch of the imagination is the United States in danger of sinking by Friday. The economy is still strong, the majority of its citizens are still content, and its political system is still admired around the world. However, just as it is necessary to ask of a company doing well with bad management how much better it could do with quality management, it is equally necessary to ask of a government doing well with bad management: How much better could the country be doing with quality management? How much worse is it going to get if present trends continue? Clearly, there are some problems quality management could help clear up.

Productivity has gone down, stress has gone up. Technological advance has speeded up, but the improvement in the standard of living has slowed down. Nothing seems to work as the people want—not the schools, the courts, the hospitals, the police, not the government on any level. There are committees and task forces and working groups struggling to find answers to all these disparate problems because Americans haven't learned yet that the problems are not disparate. It is all the same problem; we do not manage things as we should. The world market has changed around us, but we do not want to change. Rather than face new challenges and change to meet new demands, we talk of "going back to basics."

Dr. Joseph Juran, the quality expert, has no interest in going back. He told the vice president's meeting in Philadelphia that before he immigrated, the village where he was a boy in the old Austro-Hungarian Empire, now in Romania, never suffered a single power failure. Not one. It never had electricity.

As technology has changed how things get done, Americans have not changed how things get run. A quality management system is the reverse side of technological advance, and it is as essential to our future well-being as the computer. Because everything is a system, you cannot change one part without changing all parts. Even for a task as simple as word processing, you need different skills with a computer than you do with a typewriter, and the typewriter required skills that Henry Ellsworth with his quill pen never had. No one could reasonably expect that the quality revolution would not require a new system of management just as the Industrial (or Quantity) Revolution required something new. Frederick Taylor and Henry Ford and others did not devise a new system of quantity management because it was fun to do, but because it was essential when technology changed part of the system. All the other parts had to change as well.

The Industrial Revolution changed society, and there

is some evidence that society is changing again. Paul Batalden sees a massive social change occurring in health care. Camille Paglia, the writer and professor, reviewed *The Myth of Male Power* by Warren Farrell and reached this conclusion: "Farrell sees contemporary gender problems as flowing from our historical transition from an epoch ('Stage I') where survival was the basic issue to one ('Stage II') where communication and cooperation, rather than competition, are required." And she added, "He sees the killer male as a dominant Stage I type unable to adapt to Stage II economic and ethical realities." Change a few words, and the same statement could be made about quantity and quality managers.

Societal changes may become even more pronounced. Peter Drucker writes that from time to time in Western history "there occurs a sharp transformation . . . within a few short decades, society rearranges itself." He calls that period a "divide" and says we are living through one now, and that someone born in about 50 years will not be able to "even imagine the world in which their grandparents lived and into which their own parents were born." Already information and knowledge are becoming more important than traditional sources of wealth—money, real estate, and labor.

You can see the effect of knowledge and information on income. Labor Secretary Robert Reich compared weekly real earnings for workers over twenty-five years old for the period 1980 to 1991. For college graduates, wages were up 9 percent; high school graduates, down 7 percent; high school dropouts, down 14 percent. The importance of knowledge, Drucker says, is increasing faster than our ability to understand it because we don't have a theory of knowledge. "We need," he writes, "an economic theory that puts knowledge into the center of the wealth-producing process."

The Deming quality management system may not be a complete theory of economics, but with its emphasis on knowledge in management, it is an excellent place to start.

Considering what has happened in our society and our economy over the last twenty years, it is obvious that we cannot continue to do what we have been doing if we want to improve our standard of living. Americans are being beaten in international trade, we are losing wealth, and we are beginning to run out of natural resources. We don't adequately educate our youth, we have more people locked up than any other nation on earth, and Americans suffer more crimes of violence than any other people. We Americans have created what may be the world's finest health care system, but it's too expensive for some of us to use. Those are just the most obvious problems; there are others as well. Under those circumstances, it would be easy to be pessimistic, but it is equally easy to be optimistic. Kenneth F. Jacobs of the Maryland Center for Quality and Productivity says, "I am very optimistic about the spread of quality management. I think it is a subject or an idea like 'equality.' Once you get it, there is no road back."

Americans have known what to do for forty years, but it really wasn't necessary for us to change until about twenty years ago. We have spent those twenty years trying flavor-of-the-month balms and nostrums, most of which were suggested with the best intentions. Even the wasted time and the failed management techniques may be an asset. We surely know what doesn't work; perhaps we are frustrated enough to try what does. Myron Tribus attributes his optimism to Winston Churchill, the British war leader whose mother was American. Tribus quotes Churchill as saying, "You can always count on the Americans to do the right thing—after they've tried everything else."

We Americans have the capacity and the system to solve our problems, to improve how we live, how we work, and how we are governed. The Deming quality management system is not some untested, academic theory. It works in the real world, and there are examples of it across the country in all fields.

Americans have the answer. When we finally use it, we will have joined the Age of Continual Improvement.

Appendix A

◆ ◆ ◆ ◆ ◆

Ford's Statement

FORD'S MISSION

Ford Motor Company is a worldwide leader in automotive and automotive-related products and services as well as in newer industries such as aerospace, communications, and financial services. Our mission is to improve continually our products and services to meet our customers' needs, allowing us to prosper as a business and to provide a reasonable return for our stockholders, the owners of our business.

FORD'S VALUES

How we accomplish our mission is as important as the mission itself. Fundamental to success for the Company are these basic values:

• **People**—Our people are the source of our strength. They provide our corporate intelligence and determine our reputation and vitality. Involvement and teamwork are our core human values.

• **Products**—Our products are the end result of our efforts, and they should be the best in serving customers worldwide. As our products are viewed, so are we viewed.

• **Profits**—Profits are the ultimate measure of how efficiently we provide customers with the best products for their needs. Profits are required to survive and grow.

FORD'S GUIDING PRINCIPLES

• **Quality comes first**—To achieve customer satisfaction, the quality of our products and services must be our number one priority.

• **Customers are the focus of everything we do**—Our work must be done with our customers in mind, providing better products and services than our competition.

• **Continuous improvement is essential to our success**—We must strive for excellence in everything we do: in our products, in their safety and value—and in our services, our human relations, our competitiveness, and our profitability.

• **Employee involvement is our way of life**—We are a team. We must treat each other with trust and respect.

• **Dealers and suppliers are our partners**—The Company must maintain mutually beneficial relationships with dealers, suppliers, and our other business associates.

• **Integrity is never compromised**—The conduct of our Company worldwide must be pursued in a manner that is socially responsible and commands respect for its integrity and for its positive contributions to society. Our doors are open to men and women alike without discrimination and without regard to ethnic origin or personal beliefs.

Appendix B

♦ ♦ ♦ ♦ ♦

Zytec Corporate Values

Zytec is a company that competes on value; is market driven; provides superior quality and service; builds strong relationships with its customers; and provides technical excellence in its products.

We are action oriented and willing to innovate; foster integrity, autonomy and entrepreneurship; and believe in the importance of execution.

We believe in a simple form and a lean staff; the importance of people as individuals; and the development of productive employees through training and capital investment.

We focus on what we know best thereby making a fair profit on current operations to meet our obligations and perpetuate our continued growth.

GUIDELINES TO ZYTEC VALUES

Zytec manufactures products for customers that compete in a worldwide market. These customers demand quality, service and value. In order to meet these demands, we

245

must continually improve our products and services, reduce costs and build for our future.

To improve understanding of individual response to
our customer's needs, this publication will focus on Zytec
"stakeholders." A stakeholder is defined as any group or
person that is significantly interested in or impacted by
the actions of a Zytec employee.

Our key "stakeholders" are our customers, stockholders, employees, suppliers and communities.

OUR CUSTOMERS

Every Zytec employer must do everything possible to in-
sure our customers' success. We can make maximum contribution to our customers' success by providing them
with:

- quality
- on-time delivery
- competitive pricing
- frequent communication
- understanding
- integrity
- responsiveness

Zytec recognizes that these are basic rights of our customers.

Without customers, Zytec could not exist. They provide us with the funds necessary to run our business. We
are committed to providing products and services which
contribute to our customers' success. Our efforts must
focus on the impact of our goods and services on customer success.

Because our products become part of our customers' products, we become part of our customers' design and manufacturing processes. Our commitment to customer success should be demonstrated in every action and decision made which affects our customers. This focus also requires that Zytec lead in quality, cost and technology issues.

By meeting this commitment and constantly improving, we will gain and hold customer respect, loyalty and trust. In turn, these characteristics will foster long-term and cooperative relationships with our customers.

Key Words: quality, integrity, value, service, technology, listening, on time delivery, action orientation, responsiveness, partnership.

OUR STOCKHOLDERS

Investors in Zytec may expect that sufficient profit will be generated to establish and maintain a strong position in the electronics industry, finance planned growth, and provide a competitive return on investment over the long term.

By operating in an effective and efficient manner, Zytec should generate adequate profits to fund our growth and provide financial stability.

The financial resources of Zytec will be directed toward strengthening our position in the electronics industry though research and development, creative engineering, efficiency in manufacturing, innovative marketing and investments in the development of our employees.

This use of funds will provide investors with a good return on investment, resulting from reinvestment of Zytec profits.

Key Words: stability, growth, profit, return on investment.

OUR EMPLOYEES

We want Zytec employees to proudly share in Zytec's success, which results from their efforts. Zytec employees will receive full management support to help them achieve quality work, a positive work environment and personal development opportunities.

The foundation of our relationship with employees is the belief that all employees understand and accept personal responsibility for their jobs. Our employees' ability to do a quality job must not be hindered by policy, management practice, or the behavior or actions of another employee.

Every Zytec employee has a right to expect support from every other Zytec employee. In addition, each employee has an obligation to provide support to other Zytec employees.

Zytec strives to treat all employees with understanding, dignity and respect. Zytec believes in a work environment which is characterized by: competitive compensation and rewards, freedom from fear and harassment, security in employment and personal and professional development.

These characteristics will strengthen the confidence and abilities of all employees, which benefits both employees and the company.

Key Words: personal development opportunities, compensation, positive work environment, support.

OUR SUPPLIERS

We believe in treating our suppliers with integrity, dignity and respect and that by doing so, they will respond with on-time delivery, quality and cost-effective products.

It is our belief that the development of long-term relationships with our key suppliers is a vital ingredient in the success of our company. We will act to continuously improve our relationship with them. This relationship is built on integrity, single-sourcing, mutual-value engineering for quality improvement, cost reduction, long term contracts, frequent visits and accurate forecasts of future requirements.

Our supplier relationship also encompasses the concepts of short lead time, low inventory levels at both Zytec and our suppliers, a formal qualification/certification program, standard packaging, frequent deliveries and a drive to simplify the paperwork process between us.

In short, we continuously strive to perfect a Total Quality Commitment and Just-In-Time relationship with our key suppliers.

Key Words: TQC, JIT, long-term relationship, cost effectiveness, mutual engineering.

OUR COMMUNITY

Zytec will be a responsible corporate citizen in the communities in which it has facilities. Employees will be encouraged to support and participate in improving the community life in Zytec locations.

Zytec recognizes its responsibility for preserving the resources of air, water and land. We will establish and maintain attractive and functional facilities.

Through employee and corporate participation, Zytec will strive to take an active leadership role in improving the communities and environments in which our facilities and employees are located.

Furthermore, Zytec recognizes its community impact and need to provide a stable business in communities where its facilities and employees are located.

Key Words: stability, environment, participation, citizenship.

THE FUNDAMENTAL PRACTICES

There are four fundamental practices which are used at Zytec to demonstrate our commitment to our stakeholders. By practicing these, we will continuously improve our relationship with the "stakeholders" we serve. They are:

- process improvements
- training
- management principles and
- elimination of waste.

PROCESS IMPROVEMENTS

Every activity at Zytec is a process which can be measured and improved. Each employee is responsible for individual processes and through the implementation of Statistical Process Control (SPC) and Total Quality Commitment (TQC), we will streamline and improve our processes.

By being personally responsible for individual processes, each Zytec employee must critically review efforts and innovatively eliminate errors and delays. Zytec will aid employees with capabilities to improve processes, through the use of such techniques as SPC and TQC.

To succeed in today's extremely competitive world, all of us at Zytec must vigorously pursue excellence and innovation in all that we do. In short, we must not be tolerant of errors or delays and do everything in our power to eliminate their source.

Key Words: continual improvement of our processes, measured results, action orientation, SPC, TQC, innovation.

ELIMINATION OF WASTE

Waste is anything that does not add value to our process and product. In order to achieve excellence, it is imperative that waste be eliminated from our operations wherever possible.

The elements which add value to Zytec process and product are those which improve quality, reduce costs, shorten cycle times and improve yield. Waste takes many forms; the most common are excesses of space, workers, equipment and materials. We must all strive to minimize our requirements in these areas, while at the same time improving service to our customers.

Key Words: appropriate materials, labor, equipment and space.

TRAINING

To achieve continual improvement and to provide a strong base of increasingly competent people, Zytec is committed to ongoing training and development of every employee.

The cooperative effort of:

(1) individual employee;
(2) employee's manager;
(3) training department; and
(4) Zytec management

is required to fully develop employees and implement continual improvement. These four elements identify the order of responsibility for employee training. Each employee is assured, by this order, that training is tailored to his/her needs.

Each year, employee and manager should plan and prepare a development plan for the employee. This action will provide the employee with an opportunity for continual improvement.

Both internal and external training can be considered in the plan. Internal Zytec training and external education resources (e.g., degree programs, graduate studies, vo-tech, seminars) provide the foundation for employee development.

Key Words: confidence, skill, personal development, career continual improvement.

MANAGEMENT PRINCIPLES

Zytec's management philosophy is based on integrity and Deming management principles. These are used to establish a work environment in which each employee senses personal worth, is treated with dignity and respect, is delegated authority commensurate with responsibility, is free to express ideas or ask questions of anyone, and is supervised by leadership.

Management will support and exercise the utmost integrity in working with customers, stockholders, employees, suppliers and our communities.

At Zytec, we support a lean staff and a leadership style of management that fosters pride of ownership and team spirit for all employees. We strive to have decisions made by those responsible for taking the action.

One key management principle is the open-door policy which allows every employee freedom of access to any level of management without fear of retribution.

Management is expected to support continual improvement through involvement, communications, coaching and listening. Management must identify, understand and support elimination of problems.

Key Words: integrity, coaching, delegation, lean staff, open door policy.

STRIVING TO BE . . .
A WORLD-CLASS CORPORATION

Management By Planning

Just In Time

Zytec Involved People

Dr. Deming's 14 Points and Malcolm Baldrige National Quality Award Criteria

Total Quality Commitment

Statistical Process Control

Service America

Appendix C

◆ ◆ ◆ ◆ ◆

Baldrige Criteria, 1993
Categories and Subcategories

1.0 Leadership (95 points)
1.1 Senior executive leadership
1.2 Management for quality
1.3 Public responsibility for corporate citizenship

2.0 Information and Analysis (75 points)
2.1 Scope and management of quality and performance data and information
2.2 Competitive comparisons and benchmarking
2.3 Analysis and uses of company-level data

3.0 Strategic Quality Planning (60 points)
3.1 Strategic quality and company performance planning process
3.2 Quality and performance plans

4.0 Human Resource Development and Management (150 points)
4.1 Human resource planning and management
4.2 Employee involvement
4.3 Employee education and training
4.5 Employee well-being and satisfaction

5.0 Management of Process Quality (140 points)
  5.1 Design and introduction of quality products
    and services
  5.2 Process management: Product and service
    production and delivery processes
  5.3 Process management: Business processes and
    support services
  5.4 Supplier quality
  5.5 Quality assessment

6.0 Quality and Operational Results (180 points)
  6.1 Product and service quality results
  6.2 Company operational results
  6.3 Business process and support service results
  6.4 Supplier quality results

7.0 Customer Focus and Satisfaction (300 points)
  7.1 Customer expectations: Current and future
  7.2 Customer relationship management
  7.3 Commitment to customers
  7.4 Customer satisfaction determination
  7.5 Customer satisfaction results
  7.6 Customer satisfaction comparison

Acknowledgments

For our first book, *Quality or Else,* we could genuinely claim that we did not mean to do it; the book grew from a television project. We can't make that claim for *Thinking About Quality.* We did this one on purpose—or, as they say in the legal language of criminal cases, "with malice aforethought."

We are both reporters, not quality consultants, so we knew when we started that, like Blanche DuBois, we would be dependent on the kindness of strangers. Well, maybe not strangers exactly, but the many talented and busy people we have met over the years who understand what we don't. Thankfully, they went out of their way to help. They also were kind enough not to laugh at some of the questions we asked.

At Dr. Deming's office, Cecelia Kilian, his longtime secretary, provided facts and insights for us as she has since 1980. Before his death, Dr. Deming read those parts of the manuscript that apply to his management system and made suggestions for improvement, which we appreciate.

John Steward in New York City was invaluable on federal government programs and gave us the examples of successful government actions and the history of systems of work.

Linda Doherty in Washington, D.C., repeatedly explained how the Deming management system works in the Department of the Navy and how it could be applied in any organization.

Myron Tribus in Fremont, California, has made too many contributions to list. They are throughout the book, but as an example of his generosity, when he flew to London to be with his daughter for the birth of his new grandchild, he gave us his telephone number there in case we needed him. We did.

In addition to the help we've mentioned in the book, William W. Scherkenbach has always been generous with his time and explanations.

Louis Savory, an author and consultant not mentioned in the book, led us by the hand through the Baldrige criteria. Curt W. Reimann helped explain the criteria and the history of the award to us even though he knew Deming was opposed.

Reuven Frank, our former boss, is retired and no longer gives orders, but his advice is invaluable. We regard what he says as an order, even if it isn't.

At CC-M Productions in Silver Spring, Maryland, the myriad details of research were handled again by Beth Ellen Bernstein, Michael Henry Morton, and Scott Masters Stein. We prefer not to say what we put them through because the U.S. Department of Labor does have an enforcement division.

In Garner, North Carolina, Marilyn Hankin again served as "first reader," making sure that what we wrote was comprehensible. She also joined the staff as a researcher. At her suggestion, and with only a little grumbling about how it used to be done, we joined the modern age. Computer searches of data bases to find specific information were done by Denise J. Jones of Information Quest in Raleigh, North Carolina.

Our spouses, Patricia P. Dobyns and Robert W. Mason, and our adult children lived through this as much as we did, and we appreciate their forbearance. It could not have been easy.

Henry Ferris, our editor on both books, kept gently nudging us to make this more of a book than we intended, and he did not remind us of the deadlines we missed. He's kind that way.

Finally, we are indebted to you. If you had not read the book, writing it would have been meaningless. Every freshman philosopher can argue that a tree falling in a forest is silent if no one is there to hear it. There are about 45,000 books published in the United States every year. We suspect that some of them are as silent as that unheard tree.

The opinions and interpretations belong to us. Where we have got it wrong, the fault is ours.

* * * * *

Bibliography

BOOKS

Boorstin, Daniel J. *The Discoverers*. New York: Random House, 1983.

Boyer, Ernest L. *High School: A Report on Secondary Education in America*. New York: Harper & Row, 1983.

Deming, W. Edwards. *The New Economics for Industry, Government, Education*. Cambridge, Mass.: MIT Center for Advanced Engineering Study, 1993.

———. *Out of the Crisis*. Cambridge, Mass.: MIT Center for Advanced Engineering Study, 1986.

Drucker, Peter. *Post-Capitalist Society*. New York: HarperBusiness, 1993.

Frank, Reuven. *Out of Thin Air*. New York: Simon & Schuster, 1991.

Hammer, Michael, and James Champy. *Reengineering the Corporation*. New York: HarperBusiness, 1993.

Hart, Christopher W. L., and Christopher E. Bogan. *The Baldrige: What It Is, How It's Won, How to Use It to Improve Quality in Your Company*. New York: McGraw-Hill, 1992.

Kelly, Brian. *Adventures in Porkland: How Washington Wastes*

Your Money and Why They Won't Stop. New York: Villard, 1992.

Kilian, Cecelia S. *The World of W. Edwards Deming.* 2nd ed. Knoxville, Tenn.: SPC Press, 1992.

Kohn, Alfie. *No Contest: The Case Against Competition.* Boston: Houghton Mifflin, 1986.

McPherson, James M. *Battle Cry of Freedom.* New York: Oxford University Press, 1988.

Morison, Samuel Eliot. *The Oxford History of the American People.* New York: Oxford University Press, 1965.

Pirsig, Robert M. *Zen and the Art of Motorcycle Maintenance.* New York: Morrow, 1974.

Price, David E. *The Congressional Experience: A View from the Hill.* Boulder, Colo.: Westview Press, 1992.

Scherkenbach, William W. *Deming's Road to Continual Improvement.* Knoxsville, Tenn.: SPC Press, 1991.

———. *The Deming Route to Quality and Productivity.* Washington, D.C.: CEEPress Books, 1986.

Striner, Herbert E. *Regaining the Lead: Policies for Economic Growth.* New York: Praeger, 1984.

Tannen, Deborah. *You Just Don't Understand: Women and Men in Conversation.* New York: Morrow, 1990.

Walton, Mary. *Deming Management at Work.* New York: Putnam, 1990.

Wriston, Walter B. *The Twilight of Sovereignty.* New York: Scribners, 1992.

ARTICLES

"A Bullet for Teacher." *The Economist,* July 24, 1993, pp. 26ff.

"America the Cynical." *Time,* July 19, 1993, p. 17.

Altany, David. "Zytec." *Industry Week,* October 19, 1992, pp. 62ff.

————. "Cinderella with a Drawl." *Industry Week*, January 6, 1992, pp. 49ff.

Ashkenas, Ronald, and Robert Schaffer. "The Lemmings Who Love Total Quality." *New York Times*, May 3, 1992, p. F13.

Auerbach, Stuart. "Baldrige Proudly Followed the Cowboy Tradition." *Washington Post*, July 26, 1987, p. A5.

Auletta, Ken. "Opening Up the Times." *New Yorker*, June 28, 1993, pp. 55ff.

"Baldrige Award-Winning Company Files for Chapter 11." *Reuter Business Report*, January 30, 1992.

Barry, Dave. "Holey Cow." *Washington Post Magazine*, August 1, 1993, pg. 40.

"Behind the Deficit." *National Review*, February 15, 1993, p. 17.

Belkin, Lisa. "Sensing a Loss of Control, More Doctors Call It Quits." *New York Times*, March 9, 1993, p. A1.

Benac, Nancy. "Americans Ask: Doctors Make HOW Much?" *Raleigh News & Observer*, April 4, 1993, p. 1F.

Besharov, Douglas J. "Not All Single Mothers Are Created Equal." *The American Enterprise*, September-October 1992, pp. 13–17.

"Betting to Win on the Baldie Winners." *Business Week*, October 18, 1993, p. 8.

Byrne, John A. "Reengineering: Beyond the Buzzword." *Business Week*, May 24, 1993, p. 12.

Case, John. "A Company of Businesspeople." *Inc.*, April, 1993, pp. 79ff.

Christensen, Rob. "Taxpayers Burned by the Bakery That Was Never Built." *Raleigh News & Observer*, June 28, 1993, p. 3A.

Clements, Mark. "What's Wrong With Our Schools?" *Parade Magazine*, May 16, 1993, pp. 4–5.

"The Cracks in Quality." *The Economist*, April 18, 1992, p. 67.

"Database." *U.S. News & World Report*, April 26, 1993, p. 14.

Debate. "Does the Baldrige Award Really Work?" *Harvard Business Review*, January-February 1992, pp. 126ff.

"Defensive Deliveries." *Time*, February 1, 1993, p. 23.

dePaolo, Ron. "A Nation at Risk—Still." *Across the Board*, March 1993, pp. 16–22.

"Drug Prices Driving American Consumers South of the Border." *Raleigh News & Observer*, July 6, 1993, p. 2A.

"Every School Day . . ." *Time*, January 25, 1993, p. 23.

Fiske, Edward B. "The Report That Shook Up Schools." *Washington Post*, April 25, 1993, p. C7.

Forbes, Christine. "And the Winner Is: Wallace Co. Wins the 1990 Malcolm Baldrige National Quality Award." *Industrial Distribution*, February 1991, pp. 20ff.

Forest, Stephanie Anderson. "True or False: More Money Buys Better Schools." *Business Week*, August 2, 1993, pp. 62ff.

Foust, Dean. "What's Black and White and Blue and Yellow— And Less in the Red?" *Business Week*, July 12, 1993, p. 30.

Freudenheim, Milt. "Drugs Cost Less in Canada Than in U.S., Study Finds." *New York Times*, October 22, 1992, p. C1.

Fuchsberg, Gilbert. "Baldrige Awards May Be Losing Some Luster." *Wall Street Journal*, April 19, 1993.

Galo, Daniel P. "Health Care in EC Countries: A Look at All the Systems." *Europe*, April 1993, pp. 14–17.

Garvin, David A. "How the Baldrige Award Really Works." *Harvard Business Review*, November-December 1991, pp. 80–93.

Glaberson, William. "Newspapers Redefining Themselves." *New York Times*, April 26, 1993, p. C1.

Glassman, James K. "P.S.—The Budget Is a Fraud." *Raleigh News & Observer*, August 3, 1993. p. 7A.

Gorney, Cynthia. "Baldrige Killed in Fall During Rodeo Practice." *Washington Post*, July 26, 1987, p. A1.

Gross, Steve. "Zytec Cancels Offering, Cites Unsettled Market." *Minneapolis Star Tribune*, June 23, 1992, p. 3D.

Haavind, Robert. "Deming Method Made Difference for Zytec." *Electronic Business*, October 15, 1990, p. 44.

Hillkirk, John. "New Award Cites Teams with Dreams." *USA Today*, April 9–11, 1993, p. 1B.

———. "Listening to Workers Pays Off." *USA Today*, April 2, 1993, pg. 1B.

Howard, Dan. "Navy Dept. Works to Do Things Better." Letter to the Editor, *New York Times*, April 18, 1992, p. 18A.

"Hypocrites of Pork." *Newsweek*, April 12, 1993, p. 26.

"It's a Quality Show." *Raleigh News & Observer*, February 12, 1993, p. 2D.

Ivey, Mark, and John Carey. "The Ecstasy and the Agony." *Business Week*, October 21, 1991, p. 40.

Kanigel, Rachele. "For Many Doctors, the Specialty Is Anxiety." *Raleigh News & Observer*, September 6, 1992, pg. 17A.

Kennedy, Paul. "The American Prospect." *New York Review of Books*, March 4, 1993, pp. 42–53.

Kretchmar, Laurie. "Oh, the Pity of a Baldrige Award." *Fortune*, March 9, 1992, p. 153.

Leary, Warren E. "10% of Spending on Health Found Lost Through Fraud." *New York Times*, May 8, 1992, p. A8.

Levinson, Mark, and Rich Thomas. "The Roaring '90s?" *Newsweek*, February 22, 1993, pp. 28–29.

Linden, Fabian. "What MDs and Cable TV Have in Common." *Across the Board*, January-February 1993, p. 14.

Mangelsdorf, Martha E. "Ground-Zero Training." *Inc.*, February, 1993, pp. 82ff.

Marks, Jerome A. "The Productivity Program of the Bureau of Labor Statistics." *Productivity Measurement Review,* 1960.

Mathews, Jay. "Totaled Quality Management." *Washington Post,* June 6, 1993, p. H1.

———. "The Cost of Quality." *Newsweek,* September 7, 1992, pp. 48–49.

Maynard, Robert. "Why the Japanese Way Fizzled in America." *Raleigh News & Observer,* May 24, 1993, p. 9A.

Memmott, Mark. "Clinton Counsels Businesses." *USA Today,* July 27, 1993, p. 1B.

Michaels, James W. "Ph.D.s in Hypocrisy." *Forbes,* March 29, 1993, p. 50.

Mollison, Andrew. "Women's Gains from Pay Law Limited." *Atlanta Journal,* June 6, 1993, p. E1.

Moore, Stephen. "Government: America's #1 Growth Industry." IPI Policy Report 121. *Institute for Policy Innovation,* February 1993.

Navaroli, Randy. "TQL Leads to Success Aboard USS *Enterprise.*" *Navy News Service,* Washington, D.C., June 23, 1993, p. 4.

Noble, Barbara Presley. "Interpreting the Family Leave Act." *New York Times,* August 1, 1993, p. F23.

"Obstetricians Battered by Suits." *Natural Health,* March-April 1993, p. 17.

Paglia, Camille. "Challenging the Masculine Mystique." *Washington Post Book World,* July 25, 1993, p. 1.

Peck, Charles. "What Merit in Merit Pay?" *Across the Board,* June 1993, pp. 59–60.

Peirce, Neal R. "Giveaways in the Pursuit of Industry Are Out of Hand." *Raleigh News & Observer,* April 18, 1993, p. 16A.

Peterson, Susan E. "Zytec Calls on Kids, Crayons for

Calendar." *Minneapolis Star Tribune*, November 9, 1992,
p. 1D.

———. "Industry Week Praises Zytec Factory." *Minneapolis
Star Tribune*, October 17, 1992, p. 3D.

Poe, Randall, and Carol Lee Courtier. "Calling in Sick." Fast
Forward, *Across the Board*, July-August 1993, p. 5.

———. "What Training?" Fast Forward, *Across the Board*,
March, 1992, p. 5.

"The Presidential Candidates Talk Quality." *Quality Progress*,
October 1992, pp. 71–73.

"The Price of Living." *U.S. News & World Report*, June 21,
1993, p. 60.

Reich, Robert B. "Workers of the World, Get Smart." *New
York Times*, July 20, 1993, p. A15.

Reimann, Curt W. "Winning Strategies for the Malcolm
Baldrige Award." *Journal of Quality Management*, July,
1990, pp. 9–25.

Rifkin, Glenn. "Ardent Preacher of Radical Change." *New York
Times*, April 18, 1992, p. 17.

Roach, Stephen S. "The New Majority: White-Collar Jobless."
New York Times, March 14, 1993, sect. 4.

Rodger, William A. "Curt Reimann: Awarding Industry for
Progressive Management." *Washington Technology*, January
14, 1993, p. 49.

Rosenthal, Elisabeth. "Insurers Second-Guess Doctors,
Provoking Debate Over Savings." *New York Times*, January
24, 1993, p. 1.

Rothschild, Michael. "The Coming Productivity Surge." *Forbes
ASAP*, March 29, 1993, pp. 17–18.

Sacerdote, Mark. "The Board of Education Fails a Math Test."
New York Times, April 17, 1993, p. 15.

Schmuckler, Eric, ed. "Condolences." The Informer, *Forbes*,
September 30, 1991, p. 18.

"Services/Suppliers." *Oil & Gas Journal*, March 1, 1993, p. 81.

Simmons, Tim. "High School Exit Exam to Test State Too." *Raleigh News & Observer*, April 4, 1993, p. 19A.

Sixel, L. M. "Quality-Award Winner Files for Chapter 11." *Houston Chronicle*, January 30, 1992, p. 1, Business.

Swoboda, Frank. "U.N. Report: Stress Is Costing Businesses." *Business Weekly*, May 31, 1993, p. 13.

Taguchi, Genichi, and Don Clausing. "Robust Quality." *Harvard Business Review*, January-February 1990, pp. 65–75.

Taylor, Ronald A. "Health Care in America: The U.S. Searches for a Cure." *Europe*, April 1993, pp. 6–7.

"Thoughts on the Business of Life." *Forbes*, April 26, 1993, p. 416.

"Time's Up." In Brief, *The Economist*, March 13, 1993, p. 70.

Townsend, Patrick L., and Joan E. Gebhardt. "Total Quality Leadership or Partial Quality Management?" *Marine Corps Gazette*, March 1993, pp. 23–27.

"U.S. Living Standard, Productivity Still Highest Among G-7." *Challenges*, July 1993, p. 1.

Vogl, A. J. "Openers." *Across the Board*, March, 1993, p. 1.

"Waving the Quality Flag." *Far Eastern Economic Review*, July 15, 1993, p. 48.

Zurier, Steve. "Wallace Co.'s on the Mend; Financial Recovery of Industrial Distributor." *Industrial Distribution*, January 15, 1992, p. 13.

TELEVISION

"ABC World News Tonight with Peter Jennings." New York: ABC News, March 22, 1993.

"The President's Budget Address to Congress." Washington, D.C.: ABC News, February 17, 1993.

"ABC World News Tonight with Peter Jennings." New York: ABC News, October 14, 1992.

CC-M Productions. "The Deming Library," vols. 1–21. Chicago: Films, Inc., 1987–93.

PUBLIC DOCUMENTS

U.S. Congress. House. *Congressional Record*. 93rd Cong., 1st sess., July 17, 1993. H24224–228.

U.S. Congress. House. *Congressional Record*. 96th Cong., 2d sess., October 1, 1982. H8480.

U.S. Congress. House. *Congressional Record*. 100th Cong., 1st sess., August 7, 1987. H7431.

U.S. Congress. Senate. Committee on Commerce, Science, and Transportation. *Malcolm Baldrige National Quality Improvement Act of 1987: Hearing on H.R. 812.* 100th Cong., 1st. sess., August 4, 1987.

U.S. Congress. House. Committee on Science, Space, and Technology. *The National Quality Improvement Award Act of 1987: Hearing on H.R. 812.* 100th Cong., 1st sess., March 4, 1987.

U.S. Congress. House. Committee on Science and Technology. *Strategies for Exploiting American Inventiveness in the World Marketplace: Hearings.* 99th Cong., 2d sess., June 24–26, 1986. *A National Policy of Productivity Improvement.* A Statement by the National Commission on Productivity and Work Life. Washington, D.C., October 1975.

Productivity Growth: A Better Life for America. Report to the President of the United States. White House Conference on Productivity, April, 1984.

Sheridan, J. Phillip. "Case Study: Naval Aviation Supply

Office, Philadelphia." Department of the Navy, TQL
Office Fact Sheet, Washington, D.C., Summer 1992, p. 4.

Suarez, J. Gerald. *Three Experts on Quality Management: Philip
B. Crosby, W. Edwards Deming, Joseph M. Juran.*
Department of the Navy, Total Quality Leadership Office,
Washington, D.C., July 1992.

PRIVATE PUBLICATIONS

"Guidelines to Zytec Values." Zytec Corporation, Eden Prairie,
Minn., November 1991.

"Westinghouse Mission Statement." George Westinghouse
Vocational and Technical High School, Brooklyn, N.Y.,
1990.

"Contract." George Westinghouse Vocational and Technical
High School, Brooklyn, N.Y., 1990.

UNPUBLISHED

Benedict, Alan P. Letter to the author.

Doherty, Linda, J. Daniel Howard, and Denise Wells.
"Strategic Planning for Organizational Change."
Manuscript written for publication in the *Journal of
Quality and Participation.*

Gartman, Jerald B., Col. USMC (ret.). Telephone conversation
with the author.

Jacobs, Kenneth F. Conversation with the author.

Mason, Robert W. "Beliefs of a Harvard MBA." Speech,
Inspector General's Staff, U.S. State Dept., Washington,
D.C., October 1992.

Orsini, Joyce N. Memo to the author.

Reimann, Curt W. Written comments to the author.

Sears, Clifford I. *Theory I: The Five Principles of Human Behavior for Achieving Excellence*. Manuscript written for publication by Corporate International Associates, Ltd., Atlanta, 1993.

Townsend, Patrick L., and Joan E. Gebhardt. "Quality Health Care Is NOT an Oxymoron." Position paper given to the author.

Tribus, Myron. Memos to the author.

INTERVIEWEES

Ackoff, Russell L.

Batalden, Paul, M.D.

Benecke, Jeanne

Bliss, Sherwood

Deming, W. Edwards

Doherty, Linda

Downes, William

Gavoor, Mark

Giovaniello, Sal

Howard, Dan

Janssen, Dale

Martin, Vickie

Matthews, Larry

Mize, Wayne A.

Mork, Melody

Moudry, Mary

Ohmae, Kenichi

O'Malley, Pat

Orsini, Joyce

Pasqua, Paul

Peters, Ray

Quinn, Doris

Ranney, Gipsie

Rappaport, Lewis A.

Reich, Robert B.

Reimann, Curt W.

Schargel, Franklin P.

Schmidt, Ronald D.

Steel, John

Stegner, Robin

Stewart, John

Striner, Herbert E.

Sugrim, Yaesang

Tersteeg, Douglas

Tribus, Myron

Turner, Jim

Walgren, Doug

Zayas, George

Zuniga, Charles

Index